CONTENTS

THE GREAT PARENT REVOLT

The Great Parent Revolt
How Parents and Grassroots Leaders Are Fighting
Critical Race Theory in America's Schools

by Lance Izumi, Wenyuan Wu, and McKenzie Richards

December 2022

ISBN: 978-1-934276-49-5

Pacific Research Institute
P.O. Box 60485
Pasadena, CA 91116

www.pacificresearch.org

Nothing contained in this report is to be construed as necessarily reflecting the views of the Pacific Research Institute or as an attempt to thwart or aid the passage of any legislation. The views expressed remain solely the authors'. They are not endorsed by any of the authors' past or present affiliations.

THE GREAT PARENT REVOLT

How Parents and Grassroots Leaders Are Fighting Critical Race Theory in America's Schools

by Lance Izumi, Wenyuan Wu, and McKenzie Richards

PACIFIC RESEARCH INSTITUTE

INTRODUCTION

The introduction of critical race theory (CRT) and race-based instruction in schools has disrupted American classrooms from coast to coast and impacted families from every ethnic, cultural, and income background. This book tells the story of individual parents, students, and school board members who are fighting this ideological indoctrination.

To start, one must ask the question: what exactly is critical race theory? The answer is clear, but also murky and obscure.

While there is great scholarly debate, critical race theory was born in the academy and can be viewed as a variation of Marxism.

Under classical Marxism, people were separated into categories based on their economic class status. The wealthier classes were designated as the bourgeoisie, which oppressed the working-class proletariat. Under critical race theory, economic class is replaced by racial categories.

African-American author and former Princeton and Vanderbilt University political science professor Carol Swain and researcher Christopher Schorr have written, "CRT views American society and government through a Marxist analytical lens, emphasizing group power and group conflict." They observe:

> In CRT and in related fields . . . racial and other social categories substitute for economic classes. White people (but also, men, heterosexuals, and Christians) are thus defined as "oppressors" and people of color (but also, women, gays, and religious minorities) are defined as "oppressed." Given that, again, per Marxism, society and government are understood in terms of the domination of oppressed groups by oppressor groups, CRT treats racism as "the organizing principle of society." Like their ideological forebearers, CRT proponents aim to overthrow the social order on behalf of the "oppressed."[1]

"In this context," they say, "terms such as 'white supremacy' and 'institutional racism' are not restricted to historic systems such as Jim Crow or apartheid but are used to describe contemporary Western, and especially American, society."[2]

Further, "CRT asserts that slavery and racial segregation were never contrary to American values; instead, America was always and remains a white supremacist wolf cloaked in a universalistic, (classical) liberal sheep's clothing."[3]

Therefore, "Core American values such as individualism, liberty, meritocracy, property rights, and even procedural equality are viewed as expressions of white supremacy and/or fig leaves to obscure white supremacy from public view."[4]

If it seems clear what critical race theory is, then why is it so hard to detect in schools? The reason is that CRT proponents know that such a Marxist-based theory would never garner the support of a majority of the American people so they have disguised it.

Writing in *The Federalist*, Washington, DC mom Julie Barrett, noted, "The left avoids the term 'critical race theory' and instead uses terms like social justice, equity, diversity training, anti-racism, culturally responsive pedagogy, anti-bias, inclusion, and more."[5]

That is why it is impossible to put an estimate on the exact number of schools and school districts that are implementing critical race theory in the classroom.

"Students of all ages," says Barrett, "are being taught racism under the guise of equity, social justice, and the rest." She recalled:

> "Why don't you want *justice*? Don't you think *equity* and *inclusion* are a good thing?"
>
> I've had this exact conversation with the high school principal at the school two of my children attend. Yes, I want justice. Yes, I want to include people. But that's not what is going on here.
>
> What the schools are doing is making children pay for the sins of their ancestors.[6]

Unlike a specific curriculum such as the *New York Times'* 1619 Project, which caused controversy over its much criticized claim that the United States was founded when the first slaves came across the Atlantic and which had been adopted in more than 4,500 schools by 2020, Barrett points out that CRT does not always show up in schools in the form of a specified curriculum:

> Sometimes the district isn't using a specific curriculum, though. In my experience, teachers can be left to source their lessons from any resource they see fit. This is particularly dangerous, considering many school districts are hiring activist teachers, who are self-proclaimed experts in "racial education" and are usually involved with movements like Black Lives Matter.[7]

What can parents do when faced with this faceless menace? "Talk to your children," urges Barrett. "The best thing we can do is instruct our own children," she says, and, "Teach them the truth and arm them with facts about CRT so they know how to identify it in school and can report back to you."[8]

Once parents find out that CRT-inspired instruction is taking place, she recommends that parents attend school board meetings and speak, inform other parents and ask them to get involved, and post on social media.

The parents and others profiled in this book are doing just what Julie Barrett recommends. They are fighting back, whether it is at school board meetings, in court, or through elections. These brave people are ordinary Americans who have taken on the extraordinary task of defeating the most divisive doctrine to ever threaten America's children.

Other books on the topic have analyzed relevant scholarly aspects, with their authors rightfully warning the readers about the inherent contradictions of the theory's Hegelian logic, Marxist underpinnings, and illiberal impulses. Our work departs from the intellectual debates and seeks to document a grassroots movement in the United States that started in late 2020 to challenge the cultural dominance of race-based thinking and public policy making.

To accurately present this genuine movement, we profiled 13 remarkable individuals to understand their unique circumstances and motivations. These are parents, grandparents, education practitioners, students and community leaders who have been affected, directly or indirectly, by the sweeping forces of thought conformity and political indoctrination culminating in CRT's ascent in their schools and local communities.

Breaking the stereotype, these real-time, grassroots agents of change come from vastly different backgrounds and subscribe to both liberal and conservative ideological persuasions.

Among them, there are first-generation immigrants from the Middle East and Asia, whose homelands bore the marks of truly repressive political regimes. There is a college dropout of Italian descent who was dismayed by his nieces and nephews' education programs in New York's public schools and started an effective organization to help elect anti-CRT school board members. We also talked to two full-time mothers whose instincts to protect their children have led them to create national networks of fellow parents to expose and challenge ideological hijacking in K-12 education. Some are scholars and former corporate executives who have found altruistic callings to proactively engage in what they consider the fight of our generation to hold the education bureaucracy accountable.

The diversity of backgrounds and viewpoints of our interviewees show the broad-based nature of this movement. Through their activism and advocacy work, each one has demonstrated exceptional moral courage to stand up for fundamental values of equality, liberty, and freedom and for the shared future of our next generation. Almost none of them is an expert on political philosophy or social sciences but they are motivated by a common desire to stop a fringe, nihilist, and divisive dogma from preying on our society and its most fragile members: America's kids.

Our book intends to amplify their inspiring stories and by doing so give contextual human characteristics and nuances to a misreported and misunderstood movement, key points of which were activated around the same time in American living rooms and local gathering places. While these cases only represent a small portion of ordinary Americans fighting these destructive policies, these individual profiles are a faithful snapshot of the movement.

These courageous individuals are not daunted by the forces arrayed against them. They believe that they will overcome this poisonous movement and will unify our nation.

CHAPTER 1
A Scholarship Review of Critical Race Theory

In 1987, the year when one of the authors of this book was born and two decades before she made the trans-Pacific journey to America, philosopher Allan Bloom published *The Closing of the American Mind*, a literary masterpiece critiquing the higher education system in America. In it, Bloom grounded his keen observations, as a teacher "dedicated to liberal education,"[9] of contemporary cultural and ideological trends threatening the liberal orientation of education:

> Civic education turned away from concentrating on the Founding to concentrating on openness based on history and social science. There was even a general tendency to debunk the Founding, to prove the beginnings were flawed in order to license a greater openness to the new. What began in Charles Beard's Marxism and Carl Becker's

historicism became routine. We are used to
hearing the Founders charged with being
racists, murderers of Indians, representatives
of class interests.[10]

What Bloom identified as a moralistic assault on the
American political traditions of constitutional neutrality, rationalism and equality under the laws has not dissipated. The
political and cultural temptations to radicalize democratic
thought with relativism and intolerance for dissent has been
even greater in the present, with many sectors of the public life
being mobilized as change agents. The threats to a liberally
minded society extend beyond Bloom's original subject inqui-
ry-higher education and bleed into the corporate world and
public K-12 education.

The battle for ideas is most fierce and consequential in our
nation's public schools, where competing proposals for virtue,
justice, and ways of life clash with potentially life-changing
impacts on impressionable young minds.

In Cupertino, an affluent majority-immigrant city in
Northern California, third graders were forced to participate
in a math class where they had to "deconstruct" their racial and
social identities based on "power and privilege."[11] An inner-city
Philadelphia elementary school demanded that its 5th-grade
students partake in a social studies curriculum to celebrate
"Black communism" and a "Black Power Rally," while only 9
percent of the school's students can read at the grade level.[12]

This thought experiment to anchor learning in ideology,
subjugate education under indoctrination, and viciously target
dissenters is being conducted systemically. A pilot research
project surveying 44 school districts in Southern California in
late 2021 revealed the large scale of the problem. A majority
of these districts have adopted policies promoting ideologi-
cally-based racial justice, hired personnel advancing diversity,
equity and inclusion (DEI), and introduced curricula on controversial subjects such as ethnic studies and social emotional
learning. [13]

A Scholarship Review of Critical Race Theory

These initiatives are based on two central tenets: 1) Most observed adverse outcomes and disparities in educational attainment, health, and wealth in our society must be attributed to institutional or systemic racism and 2) To dismantle inequitable structures caused by racism, students and other participants must answer calls for political action, including ideological anti-racism learning, critical consciousness building, DEI learning, and so-called "action civics." In other words, the new learning paradigm is closely linked to main tenets of critical race theory, a contested and politicized hypothesis that examines all social relations, economic life, and policy outcomes through the lens of race.

Proponents of the new-age learning experience adamantly deny their connections to CRT and purposefully confuse public conservations with esoteric conceptualizations and elite talks. In San Diego Unified School District, for instance, district officials insist on every occasion that its schools are not teaching CRT, even after a civil rights complaint was launched regarding the district's mandatory employee trainings titled "White Privilege," "Critical Self-Awareness," "Anti-Racist Leadership" and "Abolitionist Teaching."[14] Ibram X. Kendi, a nationally recognized popularizer of CRT ideology, smears the opponents of CRT as bad-faith conservatives who "have buried the actual definition of critical race theory,"[15] despite the fact that the spontaneous, bottom-up reactions to the propagation of CRT in America has been demonstrably bipartisan and broad-based. Across the country, parents, private citizens and un-conforming educators have taken notice of this alarming trend.

This chapter surveys the intellectual debate on CRT and the doctrine's various crystallizations in schools and workplaces, respectively.

A Brief Literature Review on Critical Race Theory

An increasing number of American students today are being taught to recognize their skin color and obsessively define their identity by superfluous group characteristics.[16] But to satisfy the scholarly rigor required to critically examine CRT as a theoretical construct with tremendous real-life consequences, we offer a brief literature review in this section.

Emerging from the arena of American legal scholarship in the early 1980s, CRT is defined by the American Bar Association as "a practice of interrogating the role of race and racism in society that emerged in the legal academy and spread to other fields of scholarship."[17] While many observers insist that CRT is a strictly law-school academic concept[18] and that debates on CRT's impacts on the broader society should be consequently dismissed, one does not need to venture out of the pro-CRT camp to pinpoint its far-reaching implications beyond its academic origins and confines.

CRT has deep academic roots in Marxism, neo-Marxism, radical feminism, critical theory, post-modernism and constructivism. University of San Diego law professor Roy L. Brooks defined CRT as "a collection of critical stances against the existing legal order from a race-based point of view."[19] This tailored conception was then expanded by critical race theorists Richard Delgado and Jean Stefancic to include "a collection of activists and scholars interested in studying and transforming the relationship among race, racism, and power."[20] The two further explain: "Critical race theory questions the very foundations of the liberal order including equality theory, legal reasoning, Enlightenment rationalism, and neutral principles of constitutional law."[21]

Contemporary CRT scholar Kimberlé Crenshaw, who coined the term "intersectionality" as a key building block of the theory, has taken a further step to correlate CRT with an ongoing battle against white supremacy, arguing that it is "an approach to grappling with a history of white supremacy that rejects the belief that what's in the past is in the past, and that the laws and systems that grow from that past are detached from it."[22] As a pedagogy or a teaching method, CRT is "the introduction to a particular form of life," serving "in part to prepare students for dominant or subordinate positions in the existing society."[23] When applied to education, critical race theorists and authors Gloria Ladson-Billings and William F. Tate IV wrote that a critical race theory paradigm of education rejects multicultural education and aims for a "program of emancipation...to be built around the question of race first."[24]

Rooted in a prognosis of systemic racism, we have observed that CRT commands five tenets of race centrality:

1. Racism is 'embedded in the structure of society.'
2. Racism has a 'material foundation.'
3. Racism changes and develops over different times.
4. Racism is often ascribed a degree of rationality.
5. Racism has a contemporary basis.

Although CRT was first introduced as a scholarly subject of inquiry in the early 1980s, a growing number of scholars have started to debate on its effects and validity in recent years. Both its theoretical rigor and empirical values are scrutinized. According to CRT opponents and authors Helen Pluckrose and James Lindsay, CRT creates a phenomenon of people searching for "power imbalances, bigotry, and biases that it assumes must be present," which reduces everything to prejudice, "as understood under the power dynamics asserted by Theory."[25] From a perspective of linguistics, York College rhetoric professor Erec Smith tackles CRT's policy solution - anti-racism:

> Anti-racism initiatives and the narratives and ideologies that feed them result from a 'primacy of identity' that, itself, results from a strong sense of disempowerment that leads to fallacious interpretations of texts, situations, and people; an infantilization of the field, its scholars, and its students; an overemphasis of

subjectivity and self-expression over empirical and critical thought; an embrace of racial essentialism.[26]

Notably, two of the most debatable projects inspired by CRT are Kendi's anti-racism scholarship and the 1619 Project by the *New York Times*. Anti-racism imagines a dichotomous remedy to racism: "The only remedy to racist discrimination is anti-racist discrimination. The only remedy to past discrimination is present discrimination. The only remedy to present discrimination is future discrimination."[27] The 1619 Project, CRT's media debut, is a journalism project platformed by the *New York Times* and led by Nikole Hannah-Jones in 2019 to reframe America's history in the legacy of slavery and contributions of Black Americans. The 1619 Project rationalizes that American history is a story of Black struggle against white supremacy and that America's founding ideals of liberty and equality were false when they were written.[28]

Many in the intellectual community disagree with CRT's findings of structural, permanent racism and the prescription of anti-racism. A group of Black intellectuals at the "1776 Unites" consortium object to CRT's simplicity and over-determinacy. According to Columbia University English professor John McWhorter, "the heart of critical race theory is an idea that all intellectual and moral endeavor must be filtered through a commitment to overturning power differentials."[29] Carol Swain writes:

> Critical race theory says that every dysfunctional condition in black urban communities can be traced to slavery and its aftermath. There is no place for individual choice or initiative. That's the theory. But what critical race theory actually 'accomplishes' is to create anger, frustration, and despondency among persons in the victim categories, who internalize this destructive message.[30]

Leading historians Sean Wilentz, James McPherson, Gordon Wood, Victoria Bynum, and James Oakes argue that the 1619 Project reflects "a displacement of historical understanding by ideology."[31] According to academic Glenn Loury,

> What happened in 1776 — the founding of the United States — was vastly more significant for world history than what happened in 1619 — the first arrival in America of African slaves. The narrative we Blacks settle upon about the American story, the American project, is fundamentally important. Is this, basically, a good country that affords boundless opportunity to all who are fortunate enough to enjoy the privileges and bear the responsibilities of American citizenship?[32]

What is clear is that CRT is not just an ivory-tower theoretical concept limited to the halls of higher education, but is an ideological set of beliefs that has spread into K-12 classrooms under the guise of the 1619 Project and other innocuous-sounding descriptions. The following chapters will describe the extent of CRT-inspired teaching in America's public schools and what parents, students, educators, and grassroots activists are doing to combat this divisive ideology.

CHAPTER 2
Real-Life Crystallizations of Critical Race Theory

Diversity, equity, and inclusion policies, anti-racism initiatives, racial equity pledges and other similar programs can all be traced back to CRT as the ideological foundation. While CRT, with its academic nitty-gritty, was originally a scholarly subject of inquiry, its major tenets - such as race essentialism, anti-racism, lens of power and oppression, and intersectionality have created a monolithic dogma. This dogma, or the political orthodoxy so to speak, informs broader cultural and political trends attempting to reshape and reengineer our society toward illiberal group think, equal outcomes regardless of talent and merit, and collectivism. This chapter examines CRT's many shifting practices from DEI reforms to the critical ethnic studies movement and social emotional learning.

Diversity, Equity, and Inclusion

The pleasant-sounding phrase is worded to signal a benign and almost euphoretic intention to rebrand our society into a utopia where everyone gets what they need. "Diversity is where everyone is invited to the party; Equity means that everyone gets to contribute to the playlist; Inclusion means that everyone has the opportunity to dance."[33] Is it really that simple?

Take equity as an example. There is no working definition of equity that can be adequately standardized so that we are not faced with a myriad of subjective and often politicized connotations. The education establishment contends that equity is giving students what they need to succeed. But what does this mean? Which factors and actors determine the nature, direction, and scale of each student's educational needs? How do we measure success?

Equity is also engineered to replace "equality," criticized as a one-size-fits-all approach in which everyone gets the same pair of shoes. This is rather a dogmatic and simplistic understanding on a core concept of Western philosophy. Examining both legal and historical resources, one can easily deduce that equality, as the touchstone of civil rights, means equal protection, equal access, and equal treatment, on a fundamentally individual basis. Equity, on the contrary, calls for equal outcomes and political favoritism towards perceived oppressions, defined arbitrarily by one's immutable characteristics such as race and sex.

Equality is the opportunity for every student to choose which pair of shoes they want to wear, while equity means that you coerce everybody to wear the same type of shoes. "Diversity" in the DEI equation narrowly covers cosmetic diversities of skin colors and sexual orientations, but conveniently dismisses individual and viewpoint diversity. By the same token, "Inclusion" in the equation often translates into exclusion of dissenting opinions. Taken together, DEI in practice can easily morph into race-based treatment of participants in education and workplaces, crude racial proportionality and even quotas.

Most importantly, DEI is intricately connected with CRT. According to Academy District 20's DEI Initiative,

> DEI is part of a growing sociopolitical movement that is introducing contentious

transformative changes based on fringe social theory to our institutions and throughout our culture, and enacting policies with almost no resistance or checks. The terms woke and Critical race theory are often used to describe core tenets of the typical DEI program. DEI and similar efforts assert that institutions are oppressive and much of society is inherently prejudiced. This is used as explanation for disparities in the identity groups that are represented in organizations and positions. Consequently, it forces the pursuit of social justice to be the priority of organizations and incorporated into every possible aspect of its operations.[34]

In other words, CRT is touted as "a paradigm to critique and enhance the manner in which the subject of diversity is conceptualized and implemented."[35] Countless DEI statements are structured to mirror the demographics of specific institutions in the general demographics of the embedding communities, demonstrating the blatant objective to racially balance. For instance, Solana Beach Unified School District in San Diego approved a DEI policy to promote "the employment and retention of a highly qualified and diverse staff that reflects the student demographics of the community and broader society."[36]

Despite lacking empirical evidence of success and conceptual clarity, the craze of DEI is sparing no American institution, big or small. California Community Colleges, the country's largest system of higher education—and the world's third largest—is considering a sweeping regulatory proposal that would establish a set of minimum diversity, equity, inclusion, and accessibility (DEIA) standards for employee evaluation and tenure review processes. For the system, DEIA competencies mean the ability to examine and reflect "intersectionality of social identities," "multiple axes of oppression," "minoritize(d) subordination," and "equitable student outcomes."[37] A boutique agricultural program at the University of Georgia recently posted a faculty hiring notice incorporating a DEI requirement – job applicants for a scientific discipline analyzing farm field variability in crops must submit "a diversity statement describing the candidate's commitment to working toward achieving equity and enhancing diversity."[38]

A recent survey of DEI personnel at 65 U.S. universities reveals that "the average university has 45.1 people tasked with promoting diversity, equity, and inclusion."[39] UC Berkeley is reported to employ 150 professionals and 250 additional students on a $25 million annual budget to advance equity and inclusion and address "systemic inequities."[40] The DEI bureaucracy also trickles down to K-12. The empirical study on 44 school districts in Southern California discovers that 24 of these districts, including 10 elementary school districts, have official DEI policies and 30 expended public education funds on paid DEI training such as professional development sessions and curricular development.[41] Among them, Chula Vista Elementary School District has a Board Policy on "Equity and Access" in which the District pledges to "eradicate institutional bias and racism of any kind," and hire a full-time Director of Leadership Development, Equity and Access. In the same district, 53.3 percent of its students qualified for free and reduced-price meals and district-level math proficiency stood at a mediocre 52 percent in 2021.

The DEI dogma has been so entrenched and widespread that a new industry has sprung up to support its implementation. Since the beginning of the COVID-19 pandemic, the DEI marketplace has seen a 30 percent increase in job growth and amassed a jaw-dropping $8 billion in annual spending.[42] The going hourly rate for a DEI consultant to help a school develop racial literacy is $1,750.[43] Based on our observations, we have seen many school districts and other public entities follow a four-step formula to perpetuate the CRT thought experiment, often under the banner of DEI or racial equity or similar codenames:

Step 1: Identify a racial problem. In the usual case of no such issue, manufacture a racial crisis.

Step 2: Demand reforms to increase DEI, racial literacy, sensitivity, healing through policy resolutions, open statements and other formal communications.

Step 3: Hire industry consultants to conduct professional development training and other relevant activities so that teachers can effectively indoctrinate and capture students.

Step 4: Drive curricular demands for new course offerings to help accomplish DEI.

Critical Ethnic Studies

The CRT orthodoxy is not only propagated through school initiatives and programs, but also via curricular changes. In this arena, a new interdisciplinary school subject – ethnic studies – has been introduced to the American public to further the political edict of race essentialism. Nowhere else in the nation has seen a well-coordinated campaign to institutionalize ethnic studies, particularly an ideologically contrived version of it than California. As early as 2016, ethnic studies as a new teaching paradigm had taken shape when then-Gov. Jerry Brown signed AB 2016 into law, requiring that the California Department of Education develop a model curriculum in ethnic studies for the purpose of preparing students to "be global citizens with an appreciation for the contributions of multiple cultures."[44]

On March 18, 2021, the California State Board of Education (SBE) adopted its final Ethnic Studies Model Curriculum (ESMC).[45] Nearly seven months later, Gov. Gavin Newsom signed into law AB101, the state mandate requiring ethnic studies as a high school graduation requirement starting with the class of 2030.[46] These two state-level developments, coupled with a decade-long movement to introduce ethnic studies principles in K-12 classrooms at both the state and local levels, have made California the first U.S. state to endorse this contested, politicized, and highly polarizing paradigm with full force.

In spite of over 7,000 dissenting public comments, the California Department of Education approved a highly contentious model curriculum, laden with ideological jargon such as "four 'I's of oppression," "critical consciousness," "intersectionality," "double helix," and "radical healing." The finalized framework was so problematic that Californians for Equal Rights Foundation sued the state challenging the constitutionality of two particular affirmations that chant repetitively to Aztec, Mayan, and African deities.[47] The State Department of Education settled the lawsuit in a favorable agreement to the plaintiffs in which the contested chants were removed from the state curriculum.

While the state model has clear ideological leanings into critical theories and pedagogy, it is not a mandatory curriculum that must be implemented by individual school districts. Local control and autonomy, however, have created space and opportunities for a more radical version of ethnic studies, named the Liberated Ethnic Studies Model Curriculum (LESMC), to rise up as the most successful curriculum on the market.

Closely resembling a state-rejected first model, LESMC is pushed by a for-profit consulting group called "the Liberated Ethnic Studies Model Curriculum Institute" (LESMCI, formerly known as the Liberated Ethnic Studies Model Curriculum Coalition).[48] LESMCI provides consulting services targeting districts in search of: 1) Anti-racist culturally responsive training, 2) District advertisement and implementation of ethnic studies, and 3) ethnic studies professional development.

As LESMCI defines the linkages between CRT and ethnic studies:

Critical race theory is one of the many theoretical lenses used in ethnic studies. Critical race theory argues that a students' every day experience is informed by their encounters with racism. Someone with a critical race lens would reason that changing racist educational structures requires students to embrace their racialized identity and other forms of identity, including gender and/or immigration status. Since ethnic studies is an anti-racist project, students are encouraged to develop counter-stories or counter-narratives to the dominant voices in traditional curriculum.[49]

Even before AB101 was signed into law, LESMC had been endorsed by over 20 school districts in California, including Hayward Unified School District, which approved an ethnic studies framework incorporating both CRT and LESMC. Salinas Union High School signed a Memorandum of Understanding with an LESMC consultant to develop professional development service at $1,500 an hour.[50]

In January 2022, Castro Valley Unified School District Board voted for a $150,000 contract for the school district to fully engage with CRT through LESMC.[51] Other major school districts, such as Los Angeles Unified School District, San Diego Unified School District, Poway Unified School District, Santa Barbara Unified School District and Oceanside Unified School District, have also incorporated major elements of the liberated version into their course offerings on ethnic studies.

Since the beginning when the California Department of Education released the first draft of ethnic studies model curriculum, Jewish groups have lobbied the State Legislature and Gov. Newsom to resolve issues of anti-Semitism in various drafts.

In May 2022, Jewish parents and teachers in Los Angeles, represented by attorneys from Judicial Watch and the Deborah

Project, sued the Liberated Ethnic Studies Model Curriculum Consortium, the Los Angeles Unified School District and the local teachers' union for violating the Civil Rights Act and the U.S. Constitution by platforming the anti-semitic and anti-Israel liberated curriculum.[52]

While the efforts to proselytize ethnic studies have been most prolific in California, the contagion of teaching cultures and ethnicities through the lens of power v. oppression has also spread to other states such as Massachusetts and Minnesota. The most troubling issue here is that ethnic studies, corrupted by the liberated model, has become a trojan horse for CRT. In response, a cross-state coalition of grassroots organizations, nonprofits and scholars has emerged in opposition. A later chapter in this book features one key member of the coalition, the Alliance for Constructive Ethnic Studies (ACES).

Other Applications of CRT

Nearly every gatekeeper of the education deep state denies the existence of CRT in grade schools. District superintendents, school principals, teachers' union bosses and others are adamant that CRT is only a legal theory taught in higher education. This is disingenuous. One may not intuitively link race-based curricula or equity-themed programs to CRT. But most such issues can be traced back to common, dogmatic influences from CRT, a doctrine that filters our complex human condition through the prism of race and reduces social relationships to power struggles. In addition to DEI and ethnic studies, new-age educational topics including Social Emotional Learning, Restorative Justice, Culturally Relevant Pedagogy, Abolitionist Teaching, Racial Sensitivity Training, Anti-Racism and Anti-Bias Training are becoming increasingly popular in K-12 settings. Albeit pleasant-sounding and well-intentioned in some cases, all these constructs can be thoroughly corrupted by CRT through the common thread of obsession with race and racism.

With a lofty promise to help students develop a true understanding of different cultural values, beliefs and practices, Culturally Responsive Learning is thematically related to a CRT-based way of teacher education to promote critical racial and social justice.[53] Scholars in this field describe Culturally Responsive Teaching as such:

> By highlighting and critically examining moments when White racial domination has been instantiated and recreated within our own experiences, we attempt to open up a venue for imagining and re-creating teacher education in ways that are not grounded in and dedicated to perpetuating white supremacy.[54]

Social Emotional Learning (SEL), branded as an innovative learning process to advance equity, is an untested model for social justice and identity politics. According to the Collaborative for Academic, Social and Emotional Learning, a leading institute that popularizes the process on a national scale, "SEL can help address various forms of inequity and empower young people and adults to co-create thriving schools and contribute to safe, healthy, and just communities."[55] For SEL practitioners, the practice must be infused with "a racial equity lens, abolitionist lens, and others to racial justice as you name it" in order to be differentiated from white supremacy.[56]

By the same token, the paradigm of Restorative Justice, which opposes traditional punishment for collaboration and communication between perpetrator and victim, is unapologetically guided by the Neo-Marxist critical theory that treats racial disparities in punishment as evidence of systemic racism and a race-based view of our school system.[57] "Critical theory, with its insights into power, helps us to move toward more just expressions of education and restorative justice."[58] In practice, Restorative Justice is hailed as an equitable solution to the "school to prison pipeline," as a model that can finally bring "a Glory Day in Education for Non-Whites."[59]

Other CRT codenames are equally troubling. For instance, American schools and other institutions today fashionably acknowledge Systemic or Institutional Racism as a hierarchy of power and privilege baked into systems and institutions that govern our daily life, benefit the privileged groups and disadvantage the victims, almost always along racial and gender lines. Ice cream company Ben and Jerry's argues:

> Systemic racism persists in our schools, offices, court system, police departments, and elsewhere. Why? Think about it: when white people occupy most positions of decision-making power, people of color have a difficult time getting a fair shake, let alone getting ahead.[60]

For the Institute of Race Relations, "institutional racism is shown in the clear patterns of differential policing meted out on a systematic basis against black people. The whole criminal justice system then compounds those racist patterns."[61] CRT proponents then present anti-racism practices, a series of policies to oppose systemic racism and promote racial tolerance. The National Museum of African-American History and Culture advocates for anti-racism: "In the absence of making anti-racist choices, we (un)consciously uphold aspects of white supremacy, white-dominant culture, and unequal institutions and society."[62] For anti-racism guru Ibram X. Kendi,

> Being anti-racist is different for white people than it is for people of color. For white people, being anti-racist evolves with their racial identity development. They must acknowledge and understand their privilege, work to change their internalized racism, and interrupt racism when they see it. For people of color, it means recognizing how race and

racism have been internalized, and whether it has been applied to other people of color.[63]

Surprisingly, none of these aforementioned proposals consider any alternative explanations such as education workforce competitiveness, lack of family integrity, cultural degradation, community breakdown, or government policies that disincentivize productive behavior at a personal level. Without taking into account such social realities, these CRT concepts are no more than ideological vehicles to advance a nihilist and defeatist worldview against individual initiative, hard work and personal responsibility.

Parents and concerned citizens are not easily fooled, however, and they are becoming more informed about CRT and its pervasive invasion in our nation's schools. Equipped with knowledge and motivated by pure instincts to protect their children, they have emerged as a formidable bloc to check the power imbalance in our public education decision-making process, expose egregious teaching materials and practices, and demand necessary changes to bring back non-ideological education. Their decentralized efforts have been so effective that the National School Boards Association and the U.S. Department of Justice tried unsuccessfully to crack down on them in the name of fighting domestic terrorism.[64] Faced with misunderstanding from fellow citizens and smears from political heavyweights including the federal government, the protagonists of the anti-CRT movement have pledged to continue. This book seeks to recount their journeys.

CHAPTER 3
Poor, African-American, and Courageous: Gabs Clark

Plaintiffs in important court cases often come from very humble backgrounds. Linda Brown, the little girl at the center of the U.S. Supreme Court's historic *Brown v. Board of Education*[65] decision, which struck down government-sanctioned segregated public schools, was the daughter of a Topeka, Kansas minister. So, too, Gabs Clark, who has filed a federal lawsuit to strike down school-imposed critical race theory requirements, lives in poverty, but is rich in courage and principle.

When she filed her lawsuit in 2021, Clark, an African-American widowed mother of five children, lived in Las Vegas, Nevada. "We were living in a motel," she says, "because I was disabled for several years… where I was in a wheelchair…." As a result of her disability, "we'd lost everything."

"We were sleeping on the floor," she said, and "I got three outfits in my closet and we were trying to decide whether we want to buy gas or food and standing in the food pantry lines for two or three days out of the week."

She is originally from Houston. Her husband, who was White, had died when their son William, was very young. After the death of her husband, she found it very hard to afford medical care for William, who had developed a severe allergy to foliage in Texas.

"So," she recalled, "my only option was to move him to a climate where his allergies weren't going to be an issue and his asthma wasn't going to be an issue." It turned out that Las Vegas "was pretty much the only option that we had that fit our financial situation."

The move to Las Vegas really helped William health-wise, but schooling turned out to be another matter.

She enrolled William in a charter school called the Andre Agassi Preparatory Academy, which was named after the famed tennis star. Charter schools are publicly funded schools that operate independently of school districts. In 2016, however, the school was taken over by the Democracy Prep charter school network, which operates in various states across the country.

Speaking about Democracy Prep, Clark said she and other parents "were not satisfied with the way that some of the schools were operating, but we were overruled [by the school's board of directors]."

Her main concern at the time was that Democracy Prep had a very rigorous program and she worried about the social emotional impact of such a program on students. However, she was "willing to just see, just accept it, and just see how it goes."

It was during the COVID-19 pandemic, when schools like Democracy Prep used remote learning to teach students, that she started to get concerned about political bias in instruction.

As with many parents across the country, she was able to monitor what was being taught to her children during remote learning sessions, where students would use Zoom and other communication software programs to receive instruction from teachers through their home computers.

When Clark saw what her daughter Danica, who was also a student at Democracy Prep, was learning in her art class she was shocked and angered. The teacher was "talking about Black Lives Matter and I was like 'What is going on?'"

She said, "he was showing graffiti all over buildings and cars and stuff, and I was just like, 'What?'" Referring to her daughter, "This is a 12-year-old and I just was like, this is a no-no." She told her daughter to leave the class. Further, summarizing a message she wrote to the principal, Clark said:

> I don't want my daughter participating in any kind of domestic terrorism if that's alright with you. Just as a parent, I don't want my daughter to grow up to be a terrorist. I mean, I don't know what y'all like for your kids, but I don't want that for my child.

The school principal told Clark that the school did not require students to participate in activism outside the classroom, but she responded, "I don't want my kid doing it in class, either."

She contends that the school was engaging in parallel messaging, i.e., "Telling me one thing, but meaning something else," so that "the class is presented to be some wonderful thing and something that entices you," which she then discovered was "nonsense that they tell you to make you compliant."

This "parallel messaging" ended up being at the heart of her lawsuit involving her son William.

William progressed through the grades at the school until he had to take a class in fall 2020 called *Sociology of Change*, which was required for high school graduation. While the title of the course sounds innocuous, the content was far from benign.

According to University of Colorado (Colorado Springs) political science professor Joshua Dunn, who also serves as director of the university's Center for the Study of Government and the Individual, "Democracy Prep modified the school civics curriculum to place heavy emphasis on intersectionality and critical race theory."[66]

Dunn defined critical race theory as the idea that "racism is entrenched in American society and that the law works to consolidate and sustain white supremacy and privilege," while intersectionality "holds that race, gender, class, religion, and other characteristics are related and confer advantages on people if they are in the dominant group and disadvantages if they are not."[67]

Democracy Prep's new civics curriculum, according to the lawsuit that Clark would eventually file, "was not just traditional teaching about how a bill becomes law," but "was a radical transformation across the school, especially in high school, from social studies to highly controversial new approach with deeply divisive programming around race, religion, and sexuality."

The alleged purpose of the new curriculum "is to help students 'unlearn' what they know about the world, and what their parents have taught them to believe, and instead adopt a new worldview that 'fights back' against 'oppressive' social structures such as family, religion, and racial, sexual, and gender identities," with students "required to reveal and discuss their personal views and identities, in order for the teacher and other students to know who needs the most 'unlearning.'"

Thus, identity characteristics such as being White, male, heterosexual, and Christian are automatically viewed as dominant/oppressor factors, while being female, non-White, non-heterosexual, and non-Christian are viewed as submissive/oppressed factors. Oppressor "identities and beliefs are then singled out by the curriculum as inherently problematic and attacked as such."

In an analysis of Clark's case, written for the respected education publication *EducationNext*[68], Dunn found that the *Sociology of Change* course mandated "that students 'label and identify' their racial, religious, sexual, and gender identities and then determine whether 'that part of your identity has privilege or oppression attached to it.'" Further, he wrote:

The course also obligates students to label white, male, Christian, and heterosexual identities as inherently oppressive and privileged because of their social dominance. The course's teacher has labeled her own race as privileged, her gender as oppressed, her agnosticism as oppressed, and her bisexuality as both privileged and oppressed. The class content also informs the students that "REVERSE RACISM IS NOT REAL!"[69] (emphasis in original)

Yet, William reacted to the reverse-racism-is-not-real claim by saying that anybody can be a racist. That comment started such a heated discussion in the class chat room that the teacher had to cut the chat. After that incident and given the experience of her daughter in the art class, Clark said, "I started looking into this class."

She said that she "started looking through all the assignments and stuff" and made disturbing discoveries:

I saw these slides talking about intersectionality and I was like, "Okay, this is weird." And I saw the teacher disclosing all of her identities and what-not and I was just like this is weird. I don't know if I like this. And especially when she's telling kids her sexual identity. I'm just like, wow, why do we need to do this? Why do we need to know that?

Clark asked William for specific assignments and "he showed me the one assignment that set this whole [lawsuit] thing off."

The assignment, she said, asked students "to list your identities, your race, your gender, your sexual orientation, your religion, and all your stuff, like your disabilities, socio-economic level, all that whole nonsense." Certain characteristics are "dominant—those things that are privileged," while other characteristics are "submissive—those things that are oppressed."

After labeling their various identities, Clark's lawsuit would allege, "The next step was determining if 'that part of your identity has privilege or oppression attached to it," with privilege being defined as "the inherent belief in the inferiority of the oppressed group."

Further, "The lesson categorized certain racial and religious identities as inherently 'oppressive,' singling out these identities out in bold text, and instructed pupils including William who fell into these categories to accept the label 'oppressor' regardless of whether they disagreed with the pejorative characterization of their heritage, convictions, and identities."

Finally, students were broken up into groups where they were allegedly asked to answer accusatory personal questions, including, for example, "Were you surprised with the amount of privilege or oppression that you have attached to your identities?"

As Prof. Dunn pointed out, William "almost immediately protested the mandate to publicly announce and label his identities." He believed that if he had completed the exercise, he would have been making a public statement about his racial, religious, and other identity backgrounds that he felt were false and insulting to his own self-identity and his family.

Although William is half Black and half White, he has fair skin, blonde hair, and blue eyes. Despite his mixed-race background and his family's low-income status, Clark said that William was viewed as "a dirty, filthy oppressor" since "he's a straight white male, Judeo-Christian values, all of that stuff."

In contrast, her daughter, whose father is Black, and who is part of the same family unit as her half-brother William, is viewed as oppressed:

> And my daughter, she's oppressed? She's just in a submissive category, even though my daughter is more accomplished than all of my

sons and myself than all of us ever had been in our lives. My daughter got a $100,000 scholarship to the ballet academy at eight years old. We never did that. We ain't never did nothing like that. She won science fairs and all of those kind of things. She's a genius. She is 97th percentile. We ain't none of that. My daughter is. We ain't none of that, but she's in the suppressed submissive category. The oppressed one? She outsmarts us all the time. We have to just sit there and take it, but she's the one who's oppressed? No. So we said no.

So, in the irrational ideological world of intersectionality and CRT, two siblings from the same family are viewed differently—one is an oppressor, while the other is oppressed simply because of physiological characteristics.

Indeed, William and his sister were both born on Martin Luther King Day. Yet, as Clark observed: "I had two babies on the same day, one of them is Black; one of them is white; one of them is a boy; and one of them is a girl, but they come from the same mother and they look absolutely completely different, with one with blond hair and blue eyes and the other with dark hair and dark eyes."

After discovering the nature of the *Sociology of Change* course, Clark said, "we asked [the school] to let us opt out of this class, but they said no because it's a requirement."

She told the school principal, "I don't want my kid learning about critical race theory because I don't subscribe to that as an appropriate field of study for a high schooler." The principal allegedly claimed that the school did not teach CRT, but touted intersectionality. However, she pointed to a slide presentation for the course that contained a "slide with Kimberlé Crenshaw's face on it and the word 'intersectionality' at the top and it says, 'the foremost authority on critical race theory.'"

Despite her arguments, the school did not relent. According to Professor Dunn, when Clark and William "objected to the forced confessions of privilege and asked for an alternative accommodation to meet the course requirement, the school told [William] that if he did not complete the course, he would not graduate."[70]

When William refused to complete the identity assignments, he was given a D-grade, which meant that he failed the class and would not be able to graduate.

In response, Clark said: "We were really backed into the corner. They were threatening to fail my son."

Once backed into this corner, she came to the conclusion, "I don't have any other choice, I think I have to sue."

"This isn't fair," she said. The school "shouldn't be doing this to him because he doesn't want to be labeled and because he doesn't want to be discriminated against."

According to the complaint filed in the U.S. District Court for the District of Nevada, "Schools may require students to recite facts or make arguments even if the student does not like the facts or disagrees with the arguments," but schools cannot "compel a student to speak his private opinions about his personal identity in front of his teacher and classmates in a way that is antithetical to his values and beliefs, as part of an overall class that creates a hostile educational atmosphere for someone with his background and beliefs."

"That is not learning and returning facts," charges the complaint, "that is compelling speech about otherwise personal opinions," which violates the First Amendment prohibition on compelled speech.

It must be underscored that it was not only William's racial identity that made him an oppressor in the eyes of the school: "As a male, William's identities were 'malicious and unjust' and 'wrong' whether or not he was conscious of these alleged facts, and whether or not he was responsible for any acts or omissions." If he denied these characterizations, it was a sign of his "unjust privilege 'expressed as denial.'"

Further, Christianity, which is William's religion, was allegedly labeled "an example of an oppressive ideology and institution against which students should 'fight back' and 'unlearn.'" Importantly, the class materials are alleged to "make explicit the 'unlearning' is to take place in class, at the direction of the teacher."

One of the most shocking contentions in the course curriculum is the depiction of interracial families like William's. According to the allegations in the complaint:

> Families "reinforce racist/homophobic prejudices." William's deceased father was white, and he died when William was too young to know him. The teacher presentation material purports to supply substantial information as to what sort of man he was, however, and what sort of relationship he had with William's African-American mother. "Interpersonal racism is what white people do to people of color close up," one *Sociology of Change* curriculum slide declares, with examples including "beatings and harassments." Defendants do admit that not all white people are guilty of individually performing such acts, but because white people belong to a "dominant group," invidious distinctions are justified: "some people in the dominant group are not consciously oppressive . . . . Does this make it OK? No!"

And, as the complaint notes, the school conceded that the required exercises and assignments involving identity confessions had indeed occurred.

The legal issues involved in the Clarks' case are monumental. The First Amendment prohibits government from compelling speech, which the U.S. Supreme Court in *West Virginia Board of Education v. Barnette* extended to school boards and students. Yet, the school repeatedly compelled William "to proclaim in class and in assignments his race, color, sex, gender, and religious identities for which he in turn would receive official, derogatory labels."

According to the *Barnette* decision, "if there is any fixed star in our constitutional constellation, it is that no official, high or petty, can prescribe what shall be orthodox in politics, nationalism, religion, or other matters of opinion or force citizens to confess by word or act their faith therein."[71]

Also based on the First Amendment, the Clarks' complaint charged that the school engaged in viewpoint discrimination by preventing William from expressing his opinion that anyone can be a racist, thus denying his equal opportunity to deliver his viewpoint. By shutting down the Zoom chat regarding "reverse racism is not real," the school "intended to chill protected speech that the Defendants did not themselves share concerning their ideologically loaded program on race, gender, sexuality, and religion."

The lawsuit also alleges that William's Fourteenth Amendment Equal Protection Clause rights were violated. By labeling William as an oppressor because of his identity characteristics, while labeling other students as non-oppressors, the school allegedly treated William differently because of those characteristics.

Besides constitutional wrongs, the lawsuit also alleged violations of federal statutes. The Civil Rights Act of 1964, for instance, forbids discrimination based on race, color, or national origin from any entity receiving federal funding. Democracy Prep does receive federal funds. According to the lawsuit, "Defendants' behavior treated William differently than other students on account of his racial, sexual, and religious identities" thereby creating "a pervasively and persistently hostile educational environment for William."

Also, the complaint alleged that the school violated the Title IX of the federal Education Amendments of 1972 that prohibits federally funded education programs from discriminating based on sex. Again, as a male, William was compelled to profess both his sexual identity and his "oppressor" designation. He was allegedly told in class only males can commit "real life interpersonal oppression" and that "interpersonal sexism is what men do to women."

While the school contended that the court should not interfere with their curriculum and the classroom process, the court indicated that it felt very differently.

As Prof. Dunn reported, the federal judge declared at a February 2022 hearing "that Clark was 'likely to succeed on the merits' since the 'speech is likely compelled.'" Thus, "the defendants, the judge said, would therefore have to 'justify the curriculum under a strict scrutiny test,' the court's most exacting level of review, which he said the class exercises probably could not survive."[72]

The federal judge's preliminary view of the case is of immense importance. If the Clarks' lawsuit were to be successful on the constitutional grounds cited by the judge, then the entire bottom would drop out from under the CRT/intersectionality classroom indoctrination movement. Instead of haphazard and often ineffective state bans on CRT, such indoctrinating instruction and curriculum would become, in most cases, constitutionally impermissible.

Indeed, as Clark says, "legislation and all that stuff, that's all fine and good, but they're gonna find a way around that, but lawsuits last forever."

In the face of the judge's initial evaluation of the case, Democracy Prep caved. In April 2022, the school offered to expunge William's failing grade and let him opt out of the course, thus allowing him to receive his graduation diploma. This reversal by the school, however, has not stopped her from pursuing the lawsuit.

Just because the school backtracked does not mean that everything is now fine for William. As she emphasized, the school's actions have "made a mess of William's life" on so many fronts.

"He didn't get into the schools that he wanted," said Clark, and he had to quit his job because the school "piled a bunch of work on him." "He had more work than there were hours in a day," she lamented. Therefore, even though the school relented and offered to allow William to opt-out of the course, that belated action does not make up for the damage and harm that William experienced.

Clark and her legal team have amended their original complaint, to acknowledge the school's backtracking, but are proceeding forward and are demanding a declaratory judgment based on constitutional and statutory grounds and a permanent injunction against the school from engaging in unconstitutional and illegal actions. Also, the amended complaint demands a jury trial.

Clark understands the enormity of what is at stake. When the lawsuit was going to be filed, she talked to William:

> I said, "William, this is not gonna to be a little thing, son. This is gonna be a big thing. This is one of those landmark cases that is going to affect the nation, son. This is not just some regular lawsuit. Sweetheart, this is gonna be a big deal." And he was like, "how big a deal?" And I was like, "it's gonna be a big deal." He was like, "I don't want this to change my life mother" and I said "it won't change your life." But we talked about it, and we talked about it as a family. I told William, "I won't do it if you're really worried about it," and he said, "well, as long as you keep me out of the media, I can do it." And I said I can do that.

According to Clark, William said, "I don't want a whole bunch of social justice warriors banging down my door." Yet, despite that understandable apprehension, William made the courageous decision to go forward with the lawsuit.

It is ironic that in so many ways, William is a poster child for Democracy Prep's ideals. In fact, William's photo was actually on a school poster, which has since been taken down. But as Clark noted, William "did exactly what they told him to do."

"In one of the *Sociology of Change* agenda items," she recounted, "you were supposed to start a protest, even if it meant protesting something at the school and it meant protesting against them." "He did that," she said, "and they punished him for it."

It is not just the huge legal issues at stake that motivates Clark. She wants to be a role model for parents around the country to find their courage to fight back.

"I was seeing all of these parents just frozen," she observed, "with terror at the idea of pushing back on the enormity of the school system, and just the bigness of it and just the idea of pushing back." Schools can retaliate against parents in all kinds of ways, so she understands why they are "just too terrified and too paralyzed with fear."

In the end, "I just said, it has to be me."

She says, "Freedom has a cost." That cost could be parents' time, the comforts of their lifestyle, or even their jobs, but parents must "get in that parent-teacher conference, get in that school board meeting, and get some [Freedom of Information Act] requests."

Parents must realize that it is up to them to fight and to change things:

> They think somebody else is gonna do something about it. We have to get to a place in our minds where you say to yourself, nobody's coming. Nobody's coming. Just because you have these rights, if you don't fight for them, then it's like you ain't got them. You better exercise your rights. Just like any other muscle, you better exercise or it's not there. We can't keep letting people trample all over our rights and not say anything about it and not do anything about it.

"So I make a big deal about it," she emphasizes, "because those kinds of things teach the little ones to just continue to accept these things and it teaches these young ones to continue to accept people walking all over them all the time."

Parents, therefore, need to organize and band together. "Y'all get together and do something about it," she implores and advises.

She wants to "start getting small groups of parents at different schools and teach them how to organize and teach them how to do exactly what I did, so they can put together their own class-action lawsuits."

For her, "Guess what, I got a 20-year-old car with a great big giant dent in it that I have to jump into to get in; I was sleeping on the floor; and I'm broke, but I still do this because I believe in what it means to be free."

Gabs Clark is an absolutely amazing woman. She may be, in her own words, "a pissed-off mom," but she is a true superhero of freedom. Her courage, determination, and commitment to America's guiding principles should serve as an inspiration in this battle for the future of our children.

CHAPTER 4

A Student Experiences CRT in the Classroom: Joshua

It would be hard to find a more thoughtful, articulate, and pure-hearted 15-year-old than Joshua – whose name has been changed in this book for privacy.

The son of an immigrant father, and an American mother, Joshua grew up attending public school in San Francisco. The family recently moved to another Northern California city.

As a student, Joshua has literally had a front-row seat to view the transformation of the classroom from a center for learning to a racial indoctrination camp.

Joshua is very serious about his education and he notes, "the middle school I attended in San Francisco is where I really started to see a shift in the education I was receiving."

"The education started to become less and less rigorous over time; less and less intensive; and less and less focused on the actual academics," he said. This reduction in academic rigor "made me realize just how important it is to really strive for excellence and to be in a school that strives for excellence."

Looking back, Joshua observed, "The school I attended used to promote excellence and hard work, perseverance, and kindness," but now "these traditional and important values are not taught."

Specifically, in terms of reducing academic rigor, Joshua pointed out, "A few years before I attended middle school, all the honors, advanced placement, and accelerated courses were cut." Why? Answer: equity, which attempts guaranteeing the same outcomes for all students.

"Algebra was cut from my school for equity reasons," he recounted, so "we were told that we would have to go along no matter our achievement level and no matter where we were performing." For the sake of equity, "we would have to be at the same level."

Also, to promote equity, his school's policies "changed to allow students to submit late work whenever they wanted to [turn it in]" and "they started to permit the use of open-note quizzes so students weren't pressured to study." Thus, students "didn't have to memorize the knowledge that was [needed] because they said it was for equitable outcomes."

Further, his middle school "removed citizenship grades, so that no one of any race would get punished."

In his current high school, "about half the teachers that I've had offer retakes on tests, to the point where you could just flunk a first test and you don't have to study and then you could keep retaking it, and it's all in the name of equity."

"I had a teacher that had a final project in class," he remembered, "and the students were told that doing the final project was optional and we didn't have to do it if we didn't want to because of reasons of equity." The shocking reason was that "it could be white supremacy culture to make students do a final project, so it was made optional."

He says, "almost all changes are made based on the idea that equity is the most important thing." Yet, he observed, "having the perfectly same outcome for every group is pretty much wholly unrealistic."

Instead, Joshua advocates "equality," where "everyone is given the same opportunity to excel and there are opportunities to excel."

> If you have an honors or an advanced placement or an accelerated type of course or a merit-based admissions system, you're giving equality—you're giving equal opportunity to everyone to excel if they put in hard work. Every student, regardless of their race, gender, sexuality, religious background, ethnic background, or age has to put in hard work and the schools have to teach them that hard work. In terms of the resources offered equality, schools could offer tutors; they could offer clubs; and they could offer academically rigorous and accelerated programs. That gives students of color, who are clearly disproportionately falling behind, the opportunity to excel. Providing them with those opportunities is important, rather than lowering the standard of excellence for everyone.

His schools' drive to promote equity has also led to perverse results.

"I've noticed kids becoming more and more detached from the learning process," he observed, and "more unfriendly." In his own case, Joshua explained that the reduction in academic rigor has affected him:

> I used to like school very much when it valued knowledge and excellence. But now I'm typically more and more resentful because I love learning and I want to strive for excellence always. Each day becomes more and more of a challenge and more exhausting because we go to school and it's like a battleground.

The classes are no longer as academically rigorous as I need them to be and as a lot of my classmates need them to be.

As an example of how school is now no longer a place to acquire knowledge, but is instead turned into an ideological battlefield, Joshua said that he has been the target of screaming by other students.

Most recently, "I was screamed at and yelled at because I messed up accidentally on a person's preferred pronouns."

Also, "There was a name of a type of sexuality I had never heard of before," he said, and after asking about it a fellow student got upset and yelled at him in front of the whole class. "It was a very humiliating moment," he sadly recalled.

"I'm not trying to make myself the victim," he underscored, "I'm just saying that there's a more hostile attitude."

Looking at the ideological underpinnings of the instruction he has received, Joshua astutely noted, "No one's labeling them as critical race theory," but, rather, "they may label [the activity] as a privilege activity or as a social emotional learning activity."

"Most of the activities," he explained, "are not presented as being racial or racially-based, but they're still mostly focused on the vague term of 'equity.'"

Yet, despite the conscious obfuscation by the schools, it is clear that the shift in teaching has everything to do with race.

In 2019, for instance, when Joshua was about to graduate the sixth grade, he was recruited to enroll in a two-year course that was billed as a leadership and community problem-solving class. However, according to Joshua, "The two years ended up being about social issues and social-justice activism, not leadership and community."

The focus of the class frustrated Joshua because "I'm not coming to school to learn about social justice or activism," which are "far outside the classroom."

Some of the activities in the course seem straight out of a Maoist Cultural Revolution exercise. In one instance, Joshua recalled:

> When I was just 13 years old, the class participated in an activity called a privilege walk. Twenty to 25 seventh-grade middle schoolers, stood in a line in the class. Then the teacher would read out statements about privilege and if the statement applied to them, the student would take a step forward. So the first statement was, "I am a White male" and I was the only White male in that class out of all the students. So I was the only one who took a step forward, and that meant that everyone saw me stand out from the rest of the class. No one can choose their race, but happening to be White was shameful. As the activity went on, students continued to step forward for each and everything that might make them privileged. Such as statements like "My parents attended college," "My parents are not immigrants," "I am cis-gender or I am straight," or "I am Christian." Those were the type of statements, and the students continued to move forward based on their privilege. It seemed very odd and peculiar to me to be doing this type of activity. Looking back on it, it almost feels like a criminal lineup, where you have students step forward as if to apologize or be singled out for privileges that they really can't help or control.

As a complement to this privilege walk, students had to complete worksheets explaining what their privileges were. A chart was shown to students with privilege categories, including those based on race, sexuality, gender, religion, age, and the background of parents.

In addition, students had to complete an assignment called an "identity wheel." According to Joshua, "This assignment consisted of a chart in which students had to list religious affiliation, spiritual affiliation, race, ethnicity, socio-economic status, sex, gender, sexual orientation, national origin, first language, physical disabilities, developmental disabilities, emotional disabilities, and age."

"It ended up being like 16 or 17 different aspects of our identity," he said, "and the assignment infuriated me."

"I was told that I would have to share my responses on the identity wheel with one or more of my classmates," said Joshua, but, "I didn't feel comfortable and shouldn't have been required to answer many of those personal questions that are the aspects of my identity, including the socio-economic status of my family or my sexual orientation." Those personal details "shouldn't be the concern of the other students in my class and they aren't entitled to that information."

So, "if I say, 'Well, I'm straight,' then I get humiliated even more, or if I say, 'I'm upper-middle class,' then that's going to be worse for me."

"My concern is not another student's sexual orientation or their gender or their socio-economic status," he emphasized, "and another classmate's concern should not be what mine are."

In order to incentivize students, bonus points were awarded to students who shared their personal details. But Joshua would not be bribed to compromise his principles.

He said, "I told the teacher that I didn't feel comfortable doing it and I refuse to participate in this assignment." He submitted his chart with many fields left blank.

"I have nothing to be ashamed of," he said, "but it shouldn't be required of me to answer."

Not surprisingly, the assignment caused Joshua both emotional turmoil and worry:

A Student Experiences CRT in the Classroom: Joshua

So it was very uncomfortable. I was extremely angry and upset with such an assignment. And, I also have to worry academically about how is this going to affect my grade? If I don't answer some of these fields about my identity, or if I object to the teaching, is that going to negatively affect me academically in terms of the grades that I receive and the marks that I received?

Luckily, he was not marked down for leaving some fields blank.

In another exercise in the class, students were asked to draw the face of a classmate by looking at the person's face and without looking down at the paper. These students were then asked to write a reflection on the exercise. Joshua said that the exercise showed him that one does not have to be perfect to do art. The teacher then had a highly ideological response to Joshua's reflection.

According to Joshua, "The teacher said that perfectionism and the striving for perfection is part of white supremacy culture."

"So perfectionism," said Joshua, "along with paternalism, either-or thinking, and objectivity are all things that are part of white supremacy culture." These and other supposed characteristics of white supremacy culture have "no legitimate evidence basis or foundation," but were "part of the curriculum for the class."

Joshua, though, stood up to his teacher: "I told the teacher that I'm having a hard time understanding and making the connection with perfectionism, paternalism, and objectivity as ideals of white supremacy." Revealingly, "she never actually explained it" and "only provided me with a with a very short response, a very odd and very distant, disconnected response about how perfectionism values, perfect test scores, perfect results, and perfect performance are supposedly a part of white supremacy culture." However, "the connection was not made to the racial aspect of it in any way."

During the course of the class, Joshua was also asked "to step back and not participate as much in class discussions and activities and allow people of color to participate." "That was really disappointing to me," he observed, "because I just see my classmates as my classmates and I don't see them based on their race or their gender or their sexuality or religious affiliation."

And then there were the "race-and-equity circles." "Those," said Joshua, "were meant to be class discussions that allowed students to reckon with and to come to terms with their race, their identity, with sort of an underlying implication that wasn't explicitly stated that one race may be bad or less good or better than others."

These circles took time away from students attending regular classes. In a sad irony, Joshua noted, "in that English class at the time of the circles, we were literally learning about an African-American boy's experience with being falsely accused of murder." "That," he said, "would have been much more informative than a circle about race and equity that focuses on very touchy-feely kind of nonsense aspects of our race and identity."

Joshua also noted that when teachers teach anti-racism or social emotional learning, "that's not what they're trained for." More important, "that's not what students are there to learn."

Further, much of the teaching "is disguised as SEL, but a lot of the teachings are racial." Recall that proponents define social emotional learning innocuously as simply the process of developing self-awareness, self-control, and interpersonal skills that are supposed to be important for schoolwork and success in life.[73] In reality, it has been used, as Joshua points out, as a cover for race-based teaching.

One huge controversy during Joshua's time in middle school was the San Francisco school board's change in admissions policy for the city's top academic public school. The board forced the school to admit students based on a lottery system rather than on the previous merit-based system. Equity was cited as the reason for the change, said Joshua, which upset a lot of students he knew:

> I think everyone was disappointed because that was an amazing opportunity for middle-class and working-class families who couldn't afford to send their kids to a private school. Yet, [the city's top academic high school] offered a very academically accelerated opportunity for those kids. I knew White students, Asian students, and African-American and Latino students who were upset at this change because those students actually work hard and they would have gotten in on their own merits. One of the school board members was claiming that merit is racist and that the concept of merit is inherently racist. We couldn't understand that. So we were all just confused, why further separate us, instead of making it so that every student is given a quality and hardcore education. So that was something that infuriated everyone.

It was not only students who were affected by the schools' race-based ideology. Teachers, too, were victimized.

Joshua said, "I remember at my school during a training session on race, on Zoom, the teachers were asked to separate into two breakout rooms—one was for people of color and one was for White teachers." "I think that proves that often people in schools are being separated based on their race and privilege rather than integrated to have important discussions," he concluded.

San Francisco schools also recommended resources to students and their parents. One such resource, which Joshua said was "shared with my parents," was the website wokekindergarten.org[74]. The organization describes itself as "a global abolitionist early childhood ecosystem and visionary creative portal supporting children, families, educators and organizations in their commitment to abolitionist early education and pro-black and queer and trans liberation." Among other things, abolitionist teaching aims to "disrupt whiteness and other forms of oppression."[75]

The site's pedagogy tab actually has materials called "woke wonderings," "woke read alouds," and "woke word of the day."[76]

"They don't even try to hide what's happening because they're promoting their preferred resource [called wokekindergarten.org]," noted Joshua. Parents "are encouraged to partake in and convey those teachings to their children."

Also, his middle school made him "take a test called an implicit bias test." This test "basically gave us a score on how biased and racist we were."

On the test, "you look at images of European and African people and you have to match it with different words." "It was a very confusing assignment," he said, "and I showed this to my parents and they were totally infuriated at why I had to do that."

One interesting subject of controversy is the place of Asian students in the race-is-everything world of public schools.

On the one hand, said Joshua, "everyone was supportive of Asian people in terms of stopping the acts of violence that you see against them." However, Asians "get lumped in with White people."

For example, his middle school was about half Asian, "and that's partly why everyone was so disappointed when [San Francisco's top-ranked high school's] merit-based admissions were eliminated." In his observation, "Asian students in my school had the most amazing work ethic and the most amazing perseverance."

Yet, he observed, one of his teachers "made it seem like it was bad to have a good work ethic or to be supportive of meritocracy."

In the end, he believes, "I think that they're willing to kind of kick those Asian students to the curb because it's more important to seek equity for the African-American and Latino students."

When asked about what his classmates think about the race-based ideology pushed in school, Joshua gave two interesting viewpoints. On the one hand, he said, politics should not be in the classroom:

> Because all kids want is a fun experience in school and to just learn about what interests them, whether that be science and math, or art or music, you know, so [classmates] weren't generally supportive of the type of [ideological] teaching. I think students are becoming more troubled by it because they see the detrimental effects that that type of instruction is having on their ability to focus simply on their education and maybe their extracurricular activities.

He noted that only a small percentage of students chose to participate in the race-and-equity circles. However, some students do like the diversity-equity-and-inclusion and SEL emphasis, not necessarily because they support the ideology behind those pedagogies, but because "it's just fluff and touchy-feely activities where they don't really have to give their full effort." So, "for students who love to slack, that's what they like."

Unfortunately, though, the race-based ideology of his schools is starting to have an impact on students:

> I'm starting to hear comments, not frequently, but every so often, which speak negatively about White people and Asian people, such as disregarding their achievements or their work just because of their race. A classmate of mine once said that all White people are rich, and that's why she resented White people, which is absolutely not the case. There are White people

who are not in a good socio-economic and financial situation. Another student said that history and American civics do not matter to her. She didn't even want to read the Constitution because it was written by old White men.

In his view, how students react to the ideology being imposed on them "depends on how much exposure the student has to the news or different viewpoints." "If," he points out, "they've been allowed to question what they've learned and think for themselves, or if there's no discussion and opportunity for critical thinking or engagement."

On the extreme, Joshua recalled one incident when one of his fellow classmates made a comment about race-based curriculum, which started a massive classroom tumult:

> I remember describing it to some people as a disgusting and horrific outbreak of screaming ensuing from other kids in the class. A lot of other kids in the class who were yelling and tormenting and harassing the boy for a simple comment he made which had been deemed racist. He didn't say he hates people of color, he just made a simple comment questioning race-based curriculum. But the way that all civility was suddenly lost to just go after him and yell at him, I was horrified when I saw that he couldn't even speak out.

Joshua respected his classmate for standing his ground and not getting angry when everyone was attacking him. However, "It was very distressing to see and it worries me because it makes me feel that I am never going to say anything and I'm never going to express my view." Thus, fear based on the necessity to conform ideologically results in self-censorship, which is the opposite of what the learning and education experience should be all about.

In sane times, teachers would step in, restore order, and prevent the ideological bullying of students by their classmates. However, these are not normal times in which we live.

Joshua said, "teachers, especially newer teachers, they're very scared to speak out against these type of teachings and ways of going about things in education because they're afraid of losing support from the administrators, school districts, and teachers' unions, especially, which are trying to be self righteous in the name of equity on behalf of the students."

In fact, Joshua said "several teachers and students that I know, who mentioned it to me, say that they're scared about what they say for fear that they may mess up regarding someone's race or pronouns or identity."

One of the main problems with race-based ideology is that it ignores the unique circumstances of individual people. "Is it fair," says Joshua, "to tell a White person who's living in poverty or who may be homeless that they need to apologize for their privilege?" "What if they can't afford the basic essential necessities, yet everyone is taught to assume that they are privileged?"

Further, "Is it fair to tell an African-American person who is achieving at the very top of their class that society will always disadvantage them and they have no chance of succeeding?" Joshua says insightfully, "that in itself is going to be a racial stereotype against them, and it's going to discourage them."

With wisdom beyond his years, he says, "I think every person's unique individual story is what enhances our experiences and it's what makes schools a more interesting and valuable place."

Joshua says his impression of his classmates "comes not from their race or their gender, sexuality, or religion." Rather, "I don't choose my friends, or which classmates I'm going to build a bridge with, based on their race, but I choose them based on their character and the goodness of their heart."

Teaching children to "dislike a certain group will only increase negative stereotypes, and I think that includes negative stereotypes of all races." These stereotypes include "the idea is that whites are privileged and greedy, that Asians are overly smart, and that African-Americans and Latinos will never be able to achieve and that the standard must be lowered for them." Joshua says, "that's totally wrong and racist in and of itself."

"Instead," he says, "what we need to do is really encourage achievement for all people."

Looking at his own schooling and what he has experienced has taught Joshua an important lesson, which is "there's only so many years in school and you can't take anything for granted." Thus, "You can't waste any time."

Yet, the public schools are failing to prepare students academically and socially, which will have a devastating impact on young people once they enter the job market.

"I think they'll be extremely unprepared," says Joshua. So, "if you are not receiving legitimate feedback for your work because you can't get a D or an F grade, or if you're allowed to turn in work late, or if manners don't really matter because you're not allowed to get a detention or a suspension, then you're not going to be prepared for the real world."

Even worse, "to not teach hard work and to not teach a work ethic is going to be disastrous for the kids who kind of cruise along in public schools" because "later on in the workforce it's not going to be a good situation for them." That's why the schools, "from the earliest age, need to instill in kids the important values of working hard, persevering, and being kind and respectful not only to authority figures, but to your classmates and teachers."

What would his ideal classroom look like? Not the us-versus-them dichotomy set up by CRT-inspired racial ideology. Rather, says Joshua:

> I wish that everyone could be seen as a class community, rather than as separated groups, with some groups being more privileged or less good than others. I just see my classmates as

my classmates. I don't see them based on their race, or their gender, or sexuality or religious affiliation.

For such an ideal to be realized will require schools to jettison their ideological indoctrination agenda. "It's not a school's place to impose on the students any viewpoint," he emphasizes, "and I think that the best they can do is to present the facts and allow the students to decide for themselves."

Listening to Joshua, it is clear that there is more wisdom in this 15-year-old than there is in most university faculty lounges and school district bureaucracies. Our nation's policymakers would do well to heed his words.

CHAPTER 5

From Communist China's Cultural Revolution to American CRT: Xi Van Fleet

Between 1966 and 1976, the newly established People's Republic of China experienced the Chinese Cultural Revolution, a mass national movement launched by Chinese dictator Mao Zedong to seize political power from bottom up and transform the country's culture along class lines.

It resulted in millions of deaths, massacres of "counterrevolutionaries," removals of historical relics and cultural heritage, and colossal economic losses.

But what does a historical event that happened over half a century ago on the other side of the world have anything to do with America today?

As George Santayana once said, "those who cannot remember the past are condemned to repeat it."

Xi Van Fleet, the protagonist of this chapter is an unconventional American heroine, who lived through the horrors and devastations of this past and makes it her sacred mission to make more Americans aware of the important parallels between now and then.

Born in 1959, Xi was named after her birthplace Xi-an, the ancient capital city of China's Tang Dynasty (618-907 AD).

She had just turned seven when the Cultural Revolution broke out and as a result only accumulated one year of normal schooling before elementary education was paused for three years so that "everyone can contribute to socialism," a proletarian revolutionary vision of the supreme leader Mao Zedong.

Her first memory of the Cultural Revolution was big-character posters plastered everywhere in her school with revolutionary quotes denouncing people and their ideas and condemning authority figures, including teachers and school administrators.

> I was too young to read the content [of these big-character posters], but I could see the illustrations of denunciation and struggles. At first, it was only words on paper. Eventually, it got violent as elementary school kids, aged between 6 and 12, started to attack teachers.

In one incident, a young female teacher, cognizant of her appearance, was surrounded, called names and spat on for wearing a hair style that was not approved by the revolutionary Red Guards. Back then, only three hairstyles, short hair, ponytail, and pigtails, were allowed for girls.

Outside her school, the society was turned upside down – "teachers were beaten, many were killed, or committed suicide, chaos everywhere." Red guards, typically middle school or high school students answering to Mao's call for revolution, patrolled the streets in their imitation uniforms with "Red Guard" badges and operated with total immunity. "They could kill without consequences. They could do no wrong, because Mao said so."

Van Fleet recalled many moments in her neighborhood where young Red Guards raided homes of so-called anti-revolutionaries and dragged everything out of people's houses to dismantle "the Four Olds" – Old Ideas, Old Culture, Old Customs, and Old Habits:

> It was basically looting. They took everything believed to be old – furniture, family photos, books... If you resist, it is a good beating. Maybe you will get killed, and everything will still be taken away.

Struggle sessions were a common sight of those days. Red guards identified the "bad guys" with the help of the whole neighborhood, school or community, paraded them around town and organized public trials. The parades and trials were amplified with loudspeakers blasting Mao's revolutionary quotes and Chinese revolutionary songs. "It was absolutely revolutionary," she recalled.

When she graduated from high school at the age of 16, she was immediately sent to the countryside to work in the fields with peasants for three years. She was one of the 17 million Chinese youth that participated in the "Up to the Mountains and Down to the Countryside Movement," a nationwide policy declared by Mao to reeducate "privileged urban youth" through farming and harsh rural living.

Having been indoctrinated to follow orders and not think for herself, she accepted her fate: "Nobody wanted to be sent to the countryside to endure exile and hardship. But I tried to tell myself that I was just not very woke and I didn't have class consciousness."

Parents had to be very careful about not saying anything to their children who were encouraged to "rat out" anti-revolutionary behaviors and comments.

She considers herself fortunate for not aging out of the school system at the end of the Cultural Revolution. After Mao's death in 1976, China's next leader, more development and reform-minded Deng Xiaoping, reinstated the college entrance exam in 1978. As a result, she was able to go to college based on her ability, rather than her class classification or political connections, a system widely used during the revolution.

After studying English in college, she was assigned a job by the government to teach English in a teachers' college for three years. There, she experienced the onset of China's "Open and Reform," a set of policy reforms since 1978 to gradually open China's markets to the rest of the world through trade, investment and cultural exchange.

It was also at the teacher's college where she became an interpreter for traveling American teachers who were organized by churches to teach in China during summertime. She became friends with an American lady who helped her get a graduate assistantship from Western Kentucky University.

She immigrated to the United States at the age of 26. Subsequently, she obtained a degree in teaching English as a second language and two master's degrees. Upon graduation, she worked as an information specialist, first in Florida and then in Virginia for the 30 years. She quit her job in early 2022 to pursue her advocacy work full time, "to give back to this country."

Even years before the 2020 haze of race riots, she had noticed a slow transformation of American youth towards ideological indoctrination, including hating "White men," through her own experience as a mom.

Her fellow first-generation Chinese-American parents shared with her their concerns of being labeled as racists if they didn't partake in condemnation of white privilege, power and oppression. Many kids cut ties with their families because "their parents don't have the same values and therefore are racists."

For Van Fleet, the accusation of being privileged and not understanding oppression because her family life in a middle-class neighborhood is tantamount to a practical joke:

> How can you tell me, someone who suffered so much and was actually oppressed under Mao's communist rule, that I don't understand what oppression is?

Divisions at her long-time workplace appeared, where conservative co-workers became silent and the progressive ones virtually "owned the space." When she was tasked to be a member of her company's diversity committee, she realized it was déjà vu. "That was absolutely a Cultural Revolution replay here."

There are three notable parallels between what happened in China half a century ago and what could happen in an open society engulfed by an orthodoxy of group think, racial identity politics, and dichotomous social relations.

First, it is the arbitrary division of people on the basis of crude and often manufactured group characteristics. Back in the 1960s and 1970s in China, people were divided by class, into black versus red classes. The class-based division had been crystalized through a series of political campaigns prior to the Cultural Revolutions, such as a succession of land reforms and purging of capitalist elements. In general, the black class consisted of "Five Black Categories (landlords, rich farmers, counter-revolutionaries, bad elements, and right-wingers). She explains with examples:

> If you have land and you employ people to work on your land, you are a landowner and an enemy of the state. If you have land and work on the land on your own along with hired help, you're called a rich farmer and also an enemy of the state. But you're not as evil as the landowners. If you're a middle-class peasant, poor peasant or a proletariat, then you are in the Red Class.

She further explains the pernicious ramifications of class division:

> Everyone knew which class they belonged to. When they filled in official government forms, your family origin and class characteristics

were mandatory questions. Being a member of the black class, you were deprived of basic rights. That title is hereditary because you passed it down to your children, and your children's children.

Similarly, in America today, people are classified by race, a pre-determined and hereditary feature. In a developed, multi-racial country where participation in the free market and capitalism has lifted everyone up in terms of standards of living, mobility and educational attainment, the Marxist thesis of capitalist implosion and a global proletariat revolution has failed to materialize. Instead, she says, "the best way to divide America is by race, given our history with slavery, Jim Crow and segregation."

You are either an anti-racist or a racist, just like in Red China, you were either a revolutionary or a counter-revolutionary.

Americans must be alarmed by CRT, she says, with its increasing demands for American students to become warriors and change agents in the names of social justice, diversity, equity, inclusion, anti-racism, and other lofty goals unrelated to education. They are almost like today's Red Guards.

Real-life implementation of this divisive doctrine often departs from its unobjectionable and virtuous claims for an improved society free of any injustice, bias, or oppression. Some college campuses are now re-segregating into multicultural spaces that exclude "offensive" bad elements.

The Multicultural Solidarity Coalition at Arizona State University, for example, recently demanded that two White male students leave its space because "there is no such thing as 'white culture.'"[77]

Student leaders of the Multicultural Student Center and the Latinx Student Center at the University of Virginia are lobbying the university's Diversity, Equity, and Inclusion Manager to keep the University Police Department out of their safe spaces.[78]

The leaders of the Civil Rights Movement must be rolling in their graves.

In many instances, racial incidents are swiftly used to justify the divisive agenda of CRT. In summer 2020, twin sisters from Poway Unified School District in San Diego started an Instagram account to solicit and showcase instances of racial slurs, threats and microaggressions.[79] In response, the school district passed a Racial Equity & Inclusion plan and instituted two new courses on ethnic studies.

In their fervent pursuit of racial justice, these young warriors have become judge and jury, director and actor. She lamented: "this is something I thought that would never ever happen in America!"

The second key resemblance is the suppression of free speech. The fear to express one's own ideas or opinions freely and the overhanging threat of microaggression are eerily similar to the battles of "intention versus impact in China." "Anything you say can be taken as anti- or counter- revolutionary," she says, "and here, if anything you say somehow does not line up with this narrative, you are a racist."

She describes the phenomenon of name-calling as "the hat factory of communism." Back in China, during the Cultural Revolution, the hats were right-wing landowner, counter-revolutionary, traitor, capitalist… Liu Shaoqi, the Chinese president at the beginning of the revolution, got the hats of a traitor and a revisionist capitalist. He died in captivity.

In America today, the reputation-destroying hats often include white supremacist, racist, and White-adjacent enablers of white supremacy. The movement has reached a cynical high when Black conservatives such as Supreme Court Justice Clarence Thomas and one-time California gubernatorial candidate Larry Elder were each given the "white supremacist" hat.

As a result, Americans today are more likely to engage in self-censorship than just a decade ago. According to a 2022 poll by the Knight Foundation, among 10,098 Gen Z high school students surveyed, while 83 percent agree on the importance of free speech for democracy, only 19 percent feel very comfortable about voicing disagreements with ideas expressed by teachers or other students.[80]

An earlier survey of over 37,000 college students in the U.S., conducted jointly by RealClearEducation, College Pulse and the Foundation for Individual Rights in Education in 2021, found that "more than 80 percent of college students said they self-censor at least some of the time on campus, with 21 percent saying they self-censor often."[81] In general, American millennials are far more likely than older generations to accept "limiting speech offensive to minorities."[82]

The systemic chilling of free speech doesn't spare any victim. A seven-year old first-grade girl in Orange County, California was forced to make a public apology after writing "any life" on a Black Lives Matter drawing.[83]

While free expression has not been completely lost here, Van Fleet describes the situation as "so bad" that it reminds her of the Cultural Revolution. "In China, we were taught at a very young age to just shut up. It's your mouth that invites trouble."

A third prominent parallel is "reporting on others," because communists and dictators "depend on people to fight against each other." Back in China, there were "children reporting on parents, neighbors on neighbors, friends on friends, and co-workers on coworkers." The same is happening here.

A Pew Research survey released in June 2022 found that "51% of U.S. adults say calling out others on social media is more likely to hold people accountable," with the shares particularly high among Democrats (65%) and Black adults (71%).[84]

In Loudon County Public Schools where she has been a long-term resident and taxpayer, two school district programs – the Equity Ambassador program and the Bias Reporting program – have encouraged students to turn on each other and on their teachers and families. Under the Bias Reporting program, students and parents can anonymously report other students for bias, which many parents and students worry will lead to efforts to cancel students who do not support race-based instruction.

A public elementary school in Washington D.C. has introduced anti-racism lessons to its students as young as 4, asking kids to identify their "racist family members" under the section titled "How to deal with racism from loved ones." Students were told:

> Just because someone is older than you doesn't mean that they're right all of the time. Parents need to stop making excuses for that behavior if they truly believe in anti-racism.[85]

The irony is not lost that, like the Chinese Cultural Revolution, the new movement for racial justice, DEI, collective consciousness, or other euphemisms has little to do with tolerance, diversity, culture or pluralism, but much with political power. According to American journalist Richard Bernstein, this orthodoxy is:

> A universe of ambitious good intentions that has veered off the high road of respect for difference and plunged into a foggy chasm of dogmatic assertions, wishful thinking, and pseudoscientific pronouncements about race and sex.[86]

She agrees with this assessment of power being the central focus. The thirst for absolute power drove Mao to launch "the biggest and most disastrous political campaign in the history of China."

She says, the "American Marxists" today, motivated by a similar desire for control and the elimination of political dissent, have pursued the "Long March through the Institutions," a strategic vision shared by Herbert Marcuse, Antonio Gramsci, and Mao Zedong.

Deliberate institutional changes have step by step hijacked liberal designs of individual rights, equal opportunity, free speech, and critical thinking. Teachers' unions inject political agendas and activist demands into normal education policymaking through collective bargaining and terrorizing non-conforming members. For example, in 2021 the National Education Association passed a resolution supporting CRT in school curriculum.

Higher education programs such as education colleges promote invasive new pedagogies, such as critical race theory and culturally responsive teaching.

In K-12 education, she identifies an intentional disregard for teaching children about the evils of communism, resulting in an astounding ignorance:

> Eighty percent of them never heard about the Chinese Cultural Revolution. And those who have knew very little. This is by design and taken from the same book of Cultural Marxism used by Mao to rewrite history, take down statues, change school names and street names. Nothing is new under the sun. Everything that's going on here happened in China during the Cultural Revolution.

At the end of 2020, she decided that she could not "remain silent anymore" and "this is time to get involved." She overcame fears of public speaking and retaliation and stood in front of the Loudon County Public Schools Board of Education and declared at a meeting:

> I am alarmed by what is going on in our schools. You have been teaching our children to be social justice warriors, to loathe our country and history. Growing up in Mao's China, all this seems very familiar. The communist regime used the same critical theory to divide people. The only difference is they used class instead of race. During the Cultural Revolution, I witnessed the students

and teachers turn against each other. We changed school names to be politically correct. We were taught to denounce our heritage. The Red Guards destroyed everything that was not communist: old statues, books, and anything else. We were also encouraged to report on each other just like the student equity ambassador program and bias reporting system. This is indeed the American version of the Chinese Cultural Revolution. Critical race theory has its roots in Marxism. It should have no place in our schools.

Her short yet poignant speech quickly drew national attention and also skepticism. As a private person who had never been politically active, she describes being interviewed on television as a "terrifying" experience. But with her husband's encouragement, she embraced her duty to inform Americans.

The message is simple: "We Americans must wake up. We are experiencing the Cultural Revolution which aims to destroy everything that we treasure – our tradition, our institutions, our government, and our way of life."

Determined to fight, she has made it a full-time job to work with different anti-CRT organizations and to spread the message about the dangers of communism:

> I am not doing this because I read a book, or I did some kind of graduate study. This is my experience. I owe so much to this great country and it is time for me to pay back.

Her love for America was planted long ago when she worked as an interpreter in China for traveling American teachers who became her "window to the world." She recalled asking a Californian of Asian descent what America was like and was told: "this is a great place where nobody cares about what you look like."

Skeptical about this rosy, color-blind picture of a foreign land that was described as racist and imperialist in Chinese textbooks, Van Fleet came here to pursue her American Dream. Soon after, she met her husband whose small-town Kentucky family welcomed her wholeheartedly:

> Reagan once said you can go to France to become a French citizen, but you will never be French. By the contrast, this is the place for everyone. It is a total lie when they say that America is fundamentally racist!

Fast forward to the present, she jokingly says her neighborhood is "the United Nations," where people from all over the globe reside because "this country has made it possible for us to succeed."

To her fellow parents and fellow Americans, she wants them to get involved, pay attention, take control of our children's education, and empower others.

She wants Americans to see what happened in China during the Cultural Revolution, as a movie with "a beginning and an end," and to apply the history to the present. She warns everyone that the end result of pursuing CRT is predictable – "disruption and destruction of a society and the total control of the population by a few on top."

A long march back is possible, she says, to "take back control of American institutions, especially in public education." The opposition, which occupies the vast majority of the society, must take the "restoration" approach, because America has proven to be "the best experiment in the history of humankind" with superb values and principles laid out by our founding fathers. If we stop them from producing "a new generation of Marxists," we can disrupt the thought revolution in corporate boardrooms, in media, in the government and so on.

To those who are on the fence, worried about retribution or being cancelled, she wants to share some moral courage that had inspired her to join the fight not too long ago:

> You are going to be afraid that they will call you a racist. If you speak up today, you may just lose your job, your business, or some friends. That sounds really scary, right? But if you still don't speak up, the next thing you will lose is your freedom. And the next thing may be your life. You should realize that you can't just pretend nothing is happening and wish it would just go away. It won't go away. We have to get involved.

Xi Van Fleet's story of Mao's China and the Cultural Revolution was one among tens of millions of similar accounts of sufferings and misery under Marxist rule. By the same token, her journey today in America is echoed by many others whose unique yet common stories decorate the pages of this book in the proceeding chapters.

CHAPTER 6
From Growing Up Sephardic in Israel to Fighting CRT in America: Elana Fishbein

One need not have lived through Mao's cultural revolution to recognize the inherent ills that critical race theory begets in a society. Such foresight can come from many different life experiences.

This chapter is about Elana Fishbein, a Jewish-American immigrant and founder of the organization No Left Turn in Education. No Left Turn aims "to revive in American education the fundamental discipline of objective thinking by educating, empowering and engaging students, parents, and community, emphasizing the role of the parent as the primary custodian and authority of their child."

One must also understand Fishbein's background to understand why No Left Turn in Education was founded.

Elana Fishbein was born in the newly formed state of Israel. Her parents immigrated in January 1951, three years after the formation of the new State of Israel in May 1948. Traumatized from the Holocaust, Jewish people from all over the continent gathered in their ancient homeland to begin anew.

But unlike most of the Jewish people who came to Israel during the Zionist movement, her parents emigrated from Iraq. She shared, "my parents were actually those Jews that were expelled to Iraq in ancient times, biblical times, and never left."

Because of the recent formation of the Jewish state, the status of Jews in Arab countries had become very dangerous. She explained, "my parents had to flee for their lives."

When Elana's parents arrived in Israel, housing and food were in short supply. Elana's parents lived in a tent and the Israeli government instituted a food rationing program. Elana shared, "so that's how we started as a country. Survivors from the Holocaust and survivors from persecution in Muslim countries who fled to Israel with nothing."

The scarcity heightened underlying tension between the different groups of Jewish immigrants. Jews that came from Europe were known as Ashkenazi and spoke Yiddish. Jews from Arab countries, such as Fishbein's family, were known as Sephardic, and spoke the language from whichever country they emigrated from.

As she explains, "Sephardic Jews were like second-class citizens the way we were treated." As she explained, since much of the country's government was run by the Ashkenazi, "those Jews that came from Muslim countries were put mostly in what's called development towns, and public housing."

Public housing areas were distressed and full of extreme poverty. She recalled that as a child she witnessed, "the sore rotting in the streets." She lamented, "I grew up in extreme poverty and during a time of discrimination between Ashkenazi and Sephardic Jews."

Elana emphasized, "Today, Israel is very different. But that's how I grew up."

When it came time for her to begin school, she and her siblings qualified to go to a top-notch boarding school. Because of their poverty, a special government program enabled them to attend. She shared, "they provided us with clothing, everything. A lot of enrichment programs, we went to theaters, and we had lectures. I mean, it was incredible." Back then, she says, only 4 percent of Sephardic kids matriculated high school so it absolutely was a unique opportunity.

Because of the program, Elana quickly internalized how education can truly change lives. Elana used her education as a tool to get out of poverty and to understand the world so she could help other people.

After high school, Elana rebelled from the traditional path for Sephardic Jewish girls. Her community was very traditional and expected her to get married right out of high school. Instead, Elana decided to forgo marriage for the time being and join the military service.

Following her military service, Elana began studying social work at the Hebrew University. Because of her upbringing, she felt strongly that she wanted to help others stuck "in the vicious cycle of poverty and hopelessness."

Fishbein received a master's degree at Rutgers in administration policy and planning. While social work enabled her to help others at a local level, she hoped that her degree would allow her to help others at a "macro" level.

She then began a job in Philadelphia at the Jewish Federation to do just that. After starting the job, she then embarked on her Ph.D. focused on child welfare services.

After securing her Ph.D. and working in the United States for several years, Elana felt compelled to return to Israel. While in Israel, hoping to use her education to benefit her country, she resolved to get involved politically and unsuccessfully ran for the Knesset, the nation's parliament.

Soon after returning to the United States, at age 49, she married, then adopted a son from Guatemala. She then gave birth at 52 and again at 54 and decided to become a stay-at-home mom.

It was when her eldest son began first grade that she noticed the first sign of politicization going on in the schools.

Her son brought home a large poster of the West Bank. But the poster did not show the accurate geopolitical lines of the state of Israel at the time. Of course, where to draw the lines on such a map is a sensitive issue, as the conflict over the region continues to rage fiercely even today. She called the teacher and the principal to learn how her son came to receive the map.

They explained that the day her son received the poster was "professional day" at the school where various parents could come and give presentations about their jobs. One mother of Arab background decided to present. But rather than showcase her job, the mother spoke to the young children about who, in her view, should rightfully reside on the West Bank. As she put it, the presenter, "had an agenda."

Understandably, she was upset. It bothered her that the school did not recognize (or did not care) that the presenter intended to have undue political influence over impressionable young minds. Furthermore, she couldn't believe that the school was not "screening" the presenters. And rather than bringing home maps of countries thousands of miles away, she felt her son should have been bringing home maps of the state of Maryland, where he resided.

The next school incident that alarmed her was when her younger son came home talking about transgenderism. She did not feel that the topic was at all appropriate for an 8-year-old.

In February 2020, she and her husband decided they would soon move their children out of the school district in the coming school year. They recognized the politicization of the curriculum and felt that it was becoming more intense.

Just before school ended that year, as George Floyd died, and national protests erupted, the school determined to capitalize on the incident to implement a radical critical race theory curriculum.

In the letter sent out to the parents, the administrators wrote, "we need to offer more explicit lessons on equity and race for our students at this time." And that although "each class also engages in a cultural proficiency lesson; however, we realize that this is not enough." The school outlined which books they intended to teach to the elementary students over the next two days.

Although the books had varying degrees of charged political language, the most problematic was *Not My Idea: A Book About Whiteness* by Anastasia Higginbotham.

The book tells the story of a girl who sees a White police officer shoot a Black man on television and strives to understand the event. The story is meant to spark conversation about racism and white supremacy. But rather than encouraging unity and love, the radical teachings in the book would divide classrooms and families.

At the beginning of the book, the author writes, "racism is a white person's problem." And toward the end, capitalized in a bright red box are the words "whiteness is a bad deal." Young children may not understand the political complexity of such statements, resulting in unnecessary guilt for their skin color and historical events in which they did not participate. Students may believe that White kids are bad and treat one another differently.

Not My Idea: A Book About Whiteness also presents a struggle between the young girl and her mother. After implying the girl's mother is racist, the author writes, "even people you love may behave in ways that show they think they are the good ones." And that "understanding the truth takes courage, especially a painful truth about your own people, your own family."

Clearly, the author intended to instigate young White readers into questioning whether their own family is racist.

After reviewing the materials from the school district, Fishbein replied to the email saying, "we find the content enormously offensive to my family and the community. It is outrageous that the school is going to impose a lesson on the students that is supposed to make White children feel guilty for the color of their skin." She declined to allow her son to join the activity.

She continued to investigate the material's sources and she found issues which further alarmed her. She realized that if schools are teaching skewed history about their own country, it can teach skewed history about Israel as well.

She considered that "if the Whites here in this country are bad, if they are racist, violent if they are oppressive and privileged" then the flawed logic would be extended would to the status of Jews in Israel.

As a Sephardic Jew whose ancestors lived in Iraq, her skin is darker than the skin of the Ashkenazi, who came to Israel from primarily eastern European countries. But the tension and discrimination she experienced as a child no longer represents present Israel. She felt that the simplistic thinking inherent in the whiteness versus blackness language could unnecessarily reignite tension within the Jewish community. Furthermore, she knew firsthand how binary thinking as applied to race harms a society.

Worried for her sons and the other children in the district, she decided to send a lengthy follow-up letter to her school's superintendent to explain her concerns. In the letter, she told her story. She concluded the letter explaining, "the Cultural Proficiency Committee sanctioned by [the school district] approaches these real social problems with dishonesty, hypocrisy, and falsehood, which on the one hand perpetuates the despair of black communities and on the other hand causes major damage to our society as a whole."

The superintendent did not respond. With concern for the other students at the school, Elana then posted the letter to the school's Facebook parent group.

Soon after posting the letter, another parent asked the page's administrator to remove her post. Many more parents chimed in, calling Elana a racist and other offensive names. One parent even told her to, "click your heels three times like Dorothy, please." The comment implied that she should return to Israel.

Eventually, an administrator removed her post adding, "I try to allow free speech here to a certain extent, but I do agree that her message went way above that."

Despite the public abasement and restriction of her speech, other parents reached out to her privately to express their concern and displeasure with the school's new curriculum. But those parents also shared that they were too scared to speak out themselves.

That troubled her. As school ended without her receiving a response from the school or school board, and as rhetoric over the race became more extreme throughout the summer rioting, she felt compelled to "launch a movement" of her own.

It was her husband who came up with the name, "No Left Turn in Education." As he drove to pick up medicine one day, a truck blocked the road so that he could not turn left.

Before launching No Left Turn in Education, she had never attended a school board meeting and had never even met a school board member. To her, it was obvious she needed to "impact those centers of power or centers of decision making."

No Left Turn in Education was the first organization that started organizing parents to speak out at their local school board meetings against the radical curriculum changes – whether that be critical race theory, the 1619 Project, gender ideology, or changing STEM standards.

No Left Turn in Education's work centers on what they call the four "E"s – Educating, Empowering, Engaging, and Eradicating.

When it comes to educating, No Left Turn educates parents and the community through media interviews. By empowering, the organization helps mobilize parents to speak out and know what to be aware of in their local areas.

No Left Turn in Education believes in civic engagement. For example, Georgia president of No Left Turn in Education Michelle Brown made national news in April 2022. At a school board meeting, Ms. Brown read aloud explicit material from a book in the school library. The board cut her microphone off, to which Ms. Brown shouted, "don't you find the irony in that?" The book was apparently too inappropriate to be read in a public meeting, but appropriate enough to be placed on the shelf in a child's classroom.

In another incident, the organization discovered[87] that North Carolina education officials scrubbed critical race theory linked words to avoid backlash from the curriculum they were adopting.

After initially denying knowledge of the materials, No Left Turn in Education filed public records requests and found that the district was indeed aware of them, and ordered their removal from the district's website to hide them from the public.

In a Missouri school district[88], No Left Turn in Education protested a new proposed policy which would deny requests by parents/guardians to be informed prior to these discussions, be present during the discussions, or prohibit conversations between a student and staff members." They ultimately found that 213 school districts in Missouri had already adopted the identical proposed policy. In their view, the policy could have too much overreach in regard to conversations about race and gender which are potentially inappropriate topics between students and teachers.

When it comes to eradicating harmful curricula, No Left Turn in Education provided the first model legislation on the website to ban critical race theory in schools. The organization's volunteers take the model legislation with them when they meet with state legislators.

Some activists responding to critical race theory may disagree with the approach to ban the curriculum, and instead advocate for transparency or curriculum replacement. Others criticize saying that No Left Turn in Education seeks to ban books.

Fishbein disagrees saying:

> We're not banning books. People can go and get them, online, in bookstores, or whatever. But what we are saying is that there are certain books and materials that are just horrendous...We are against books that are imposing the orthodoxy of the radical left. We are against books that are sexualizing our kids

as young as three and four and five years old and we are against books that teach kids to judge others based on the color of their skin, or any immutable characteristic. We're against books that aim to turn our kids into social justice warriors. We're against books that are promoting hatred of America...and we're against books that teach the false narrative of the 1619 Project.

When it comes to pushing back against critical race theory, she recognizes that "this is not an overnight thing" but there are a lot of committed people around the country who want to work together to protect kids from harmful teachings.

CHAPTER 7

In the Footsteps of Gandhi, a Muslim Woman Talks about Race In America: Asra Nomani

If ever there was a person who defied the stereotype of what an opponent of critical race theory looks like it is Asra Nomani, who has become one of the country's key parent leaders fighting race ideology in schools.

Born in India, she said, "my mom and dad both come from conservative Muslim families."

Her mother grew up in the homes of relatives after her father died when she was very young. According to Nomani, "My mom remembers that she went to a religious family and they sent all their kids to the madrassa or the Muslim religious school." "My mom saw how strict and dogmatic and rigid that family culture was and said to herself as a little girl, just about the age of seven, that's not what she wanted."

She says, "my mom literally had to wear the face veil as a young Muslim girl," but one day she took the veil off at school "causing a great ruckus in the family."

Her father "lived through the Bengal famine in the early 1940s that stretched into the city of Hyderabad where he lived." "And to this day," she says, "tears come to his eyes as he remembers standing in line for the aid that had come from America as food."

When India achieved independence from Britain, she said that her mother "remembers so vividly the day in August 1947 when freedom came to the brown-skinned Indians."

"My dad," she says, "literally marched with Mahatma Gandhi" for India's freedom.

While her mother was receiving a Cadbury chocolate bar from the nuns at her school to celebrate India's independence, she says, "my dad was watching the British flag come down and the Indian flag went up."

Says Nomani, her mother and father "grew up literally under the yoke of white supremacy." "Those are the parents to whom I was born," she says, and "that is the post-colonial India into which I was born as first generation."

"My mom and dad valued education in both their paths," she said, "and my dad got a master's degree in India."

One day, one of her father's university teachers showed slides of his trip to America, including a photo of a pink flamingo. He thought the bird was so beautiful that he wanted to see one for himself and applied for a teaching fellowship in Kansas.

Although he did not see any pink flamingoes in Kansas, he was amazed by the equality he saw in America compared to India's historical caste system and he returned to India with these lessons.

The entire family would later return to America.

"I came [to America] knowing no English," she said, "I was four." She attended a local elementary school named after Martin Luther King, Jr.

When she was 10, her family moved to West Virginia. In West Virginia, which had many impoverished areas, she saw White families struggling. Witnessing their struggles, "it informed me to reject this kind of binary about White is bad and

Black is good in this critical race theory that people are trying to thrust upon us."

In high school, "I ended up falling in love with journalism." Eventually, she would be hired as a reporter for *The Wall Street Journal*. She worked at the newspaper for 15 years, during which time her best friend was her fellow reporter Daniel Pearl, a Jewish-American who was the paper's bureau chief for South Asia.

Pearl, sadly, is remembered now for being kidnapped by radical Islamic terrorists in 2002 in Pakistan. Eventually, his captors would behead him.

On the day of Pearl's kidnapping, she recalled, "the entire trajectory of my life changed and I went from being this reporter observing reality to fighting for justice for my friend."

Pearl's kidnappers made a video of his beheading, which Asra watched years later, "and in it I saw poor Danny dehumanized by his captors because of his identity." "They made him talk about his Jewish identity," she said, and how "his father and his grandparents are rooted in Israel."

During the time of Pearl's kidnapping, she found out that she was pregnant. Describing this personal trauma, she said, "in my culture being an unwed mother is not a sin, but a crime in Muslim countries."

"The father of my son abandoned us, "she said, "I literally thought [her baby] was going to have scars on his face because I had swallowed so many tears during my pregnancy." When her son was born without any physical scars, she thought, "I cannot scar him emotionally, I cannot have him absorb shame as part of his growth."

This epiphany, she says informed "the passion in my heart when I speak about these children that are being shamed, like [Gabs Clark's] son, like the White children, the Asian children, and the Black children." "I know the suffering that comes from living in shame," she said, because "I absorbed the shame and [endured] depression and anxiety."

It was with her son's birth, however, that she was freed from her shame. She went on a pilgrimage to Mecca in Saudi Arabia "with my son on my chest." She realized "the truth of human beings and children, especially, is their intrinsic value, their intrinsic worth, their intrinsic humanity." "All of this nonsense," such as valuing people by their racial identity, "speaks to the dehumanization of people."

She was shocked that in Mecca there was no segregation based on gender, "So I actually prayed shoulder to shoulder next to my father, which is something that I cannot do in just about any mosque in the world, and I realized coming back that when you do not allow equality in the public space, or any space, it spills over into everything—education, legal rights, personal law, all of these injustices." As a result of this realization, she became an advocate for women's rights.

She ended up writing a highly acclaimed book entitled *Standing Alone in Mecca*.

As the years went on, her son became an excellent student. Nomani had settled in Virginia and her son was eventually accepted to Fairfax County's Thomas Jefferson High School for Science and Technology (colloquially known as "TJ"), which is recognized as one of the best public high schools in America.

Her son entered TJ under a merit-based and race-blind admissions system that at the time consisted of a standardized entrance test, grade-point average, completion of certain math courses, and teacher recommendations.

When her son was admitted to TJ, she said, "he was celebrating, walking into that domed school building, not as a thing of ego, but of just hard work and a symbol of our journey."

At TJ, she found "a diversity I had never experienced in America." "I learned the Chinese New Year festival," she recalled, "and had so many good conversations with parents who were immigrants like me and it was so exciting."

Then everything changed. In 2020, the Fairfax County Public Schools completely overhauled the admissions system. Why would the school district want to change a system that had resulted in its school being rated among the top in the country? Answer: too many Asians.

Prior to the change in the admissions system, seven out of 10 TJ students were Asian-Americans. Writing in an op-ed article for *USA Today*, she observed that many of those Asian-American parents were "immigrants, like me, who believe in the idea of an American Dream, in which people advance in life with hard work."[89]

"County school officials," she said, "set out to correct the supposedly problematic over-representation of Asian-American students at TJ by watering down the strict admission standards." The former merit-based system, including the standardized test, was replaced "with a new process that includes completing an essay and a 'Student Portrait Sheet' that reveals 'experience factors' like language spoken at home and family wealth."

Significantly, multiple members of the school board said that they were uncomfortable with the speed with which the changes were adopted and the inadequate opportunity for parent and community input.

Further, "Although the new process states it will 'use only race-neutral methods,' in practice this subjective set of standards allows them to pick and choose the students they prefer to achieve their desired racial balance and keep out too many Asian-American students."

The new admissions system also capped the number of students that could enter TJ from the district's 23 middle schools.[90] Importantly, three of those middle schools, which typically accounted for most of TJ's admissions, had higher numbers of Asian-American students than the other middle schools. So, capping the number of students who could enter TJ from those three schools effectively put a cap on the number of Asian-American students who could enter TJ.

"Many Asian-American families, like mine," she noted, "have worked hard and sacrificed to prepare their children to meet the rigors of the test and the TJ curriculum" and "protested this weakening of standards—in part because it was clearly aimed at reducing our numbers in the student body, but just as importantly because it would degrade TJ's long tradition of advanced learning."

Why would county and school officials want to target Asian-American students, whose only crime was to work hard and achieve academic excellence?

"To understand what's behind this conflict," she wrote, "look no further than the controversial ideology of critical race theory, which praises or blames members of a particular race solely because they happen to be that race and seeks to interpret all forms of perceived injustice through a racial lens."

"This ideology," she says, "has swept through America's educational system at every level and is erasing our different narratives as Asian-Americans from different backgrounds and—to our shock—marginalizing our children and us."

"The ugly truth about critical race theory," she underscores, "is that it inevitably seeks to fight racial hierarchies by instituting new forms of racial hierarchies, and Asian-American parents are increasingly taking notice."

Because of the impetus of critical race theory, she believes, TJ leaders "repeatedly put the focus squarely on racial balance at the school and the number of Black and Brown children at TJ, somehow overlooking the fact that the many students of Indian descent are 'Brown.'"

"We don't begrudge any child who is qualified and meets the previous rigorous criteria from attending TJ," but, she emphasizes, "Nor should our children be begrudged the opportunity simply because of their Asian heritage."

Unfortunately, however, TJ's new subjective admissions system, just like the subjective admissions system used by Harvard University, which is the subject of a lawsuit before the U.S. Supreme Court, resulted in a drastic reduction in the proportion of Asian-American students at the school.

Asian-American admittees fell from 73 percent under the merit-based system to 54 percent under the new subjective system. "The percentage of blacks and Hispanics increased," Nomani observed in an interview with *City Journal*, "as it also did for white students."[91]

A Muslim Woman Talks about Race in America: Asra Nomani

She told the publication, "This is a purge against Asian-American students by Fairfax County Public Schools."

She compares the discrimination that Asian-Americans are experiencing today in education with the open bigotry against Jews early in the 20th century:

> Asian-American students in 2021 are experiencing the same type of discrimination and bigotry that Jewish American students faced a century ago. In 1922, Harvard University President Abbott Lawrence lamented to alumni and donors who complained about the number of Jewish students that he had "foreseen the peril of having too large a number of an alien race, and had tried to prevent it."
>
> Most of us recoil at such rhetoric today, and rightfully so. But Lawrence's perspective on Jews a century ago is similar to how today's elite educational administrators discuss Asian-Americans. The only difference is that today they wrap their prejudice in the soothing and noble-sounding therapeutic language of diversity.

TJ also insulted parents by sending out an email asking them to check their privilege. That message, she said, "hit us over the head like with a hammer." She said, "our jaws dropped, our hearts dropped."

She pointed out that there were parents at the school who had survived the genocidal Cultural Revolution in Communist China and parents who had survived communism in Eastern Europe. "This is so dehumanizing," she said.

Because of this open discrimination by the school, she became an education activist. She started to meet with other parents, attended school board meetings, and appealed to school board members to reconsider their policy decisions.

"Little did I know," she said, "that they were captive to critical race theory." She found out that the system had even booked CRT guru Ibram Kendi at a hefty price.

When she found out, through a phone call with an Associated Press reporter, that then-Democrat Gov. Ralph Northam's education secretary had started a task force that would impact admissions to TJ, she said, "I'm not just going to be a parent, I'm going to investigate."

Not only did she find the minutes of the education secretary's meeting, she started a Substack account, which became her platform. She also helped start an organization of parents called the Coalition for TJ, which grew to hundreds of members.

While the Coalition for TJ fought "for our rights as Asian families," she noted, "even the non-Asian families understood that this was a fight for equal rights in America."

Among the members of the Coalition are people like Yuyan Zhou, who had two children attending TJ, and who marched in Tiananmen Square against the oppression of the Communist Chinese government. Yuyan came to the United States with a belief that opportunities should be open to everyone regardless of their race.

Harry Jackson, another member of the Coalition, is father to one of the six African-American students admitted to TJ prior to the change in the admissions system. He believes that rather than changing the admissions system and discriminating against Asian students, schools should improve the academic pipeline for African-American and Hispanic students.

"I am grounded in liberal politics," she says, and "I voted Democrat all my life and I'm a feminist." "I know the slogans of liberalism," she explained, "and they broke every single one of them," and the key one that they broke "is talking about us without us."

Besides changing the admissions system, TJ leaders wanted to get rid of the school's "Colonials" nickname because it supposedly symbolized colonialism, "Like most of our families, my parents had survived colonialism," she said, "and we saw

A Muslim Woman Talks about Race in America: Asra Nomani

the Colonials as heroes who had actually taken off the yoke of the British."

Supporters of the new admissions system accused Nomani and her fellow Asian parents as being White-adjacent and resource hoarders. "Their weapon against us was shame," she said, "and it was always understood to be ashamed as Asians."

But in the face of such shaming tactics, Nomani said, "we were unapologetic."

Eventually, it became clear that the pro-CRT-influenced school board and county school system would not budge from their ideological commitment to discriminate against Asian-American students in favor of blatant racial balancing. The Coalition for TJ, therefore, decided to file a lawsuit against the Fairfax County School Board in the United States District Court for Eastern Virginia.

The Pacific Legal Foundation (PLF), a non-profit legal organization that fights for individual liberty and against government overreach, agreed to represent the Coalition.

According to PLF, not only did school district officials make "no secret that their clear and unequivocal objective is to reduce the number of Asian-American students at TJ," but there is "no evidence the district considered any race-neutral alternative, like creating additional STEM high schools or providing greater access to standardized testing prep without middle school quotas."

In February 2022, federal judge Claude Hilton ruled decisively for the Coalition for TJ.

Hilton found, "Board member communications show a consensus that, in their view, the racial makeup of TJ was problematic and should be changed."[92]

Indeed, "emails and text messages between Board members and high-ranking FCPS officials leave no material dispute that, at least in part, the purpose of the Board's admissions overhaul was to change the racial makeup to TJ to the detriment of Asian-Americans."[93]

"The Board's overhaul of TJ admissions," wrote Hilton, "has had, and will have, a substantial disparate impact on

Asian-American applicants to TJ," and "disparate impact is the starting point for determining whether the Board acted with discriminatory intent."[94]

Under TJ's new policy, the proportion of offers of admission made to Asian-Americans had fallen by 19 percent. In view of this drop, Hilton said, "The undisputed evidence demonstrates precisely how the Board's actions caused, and will continue to cause a substantial racial impact," meaning that the school board "instituted a system that does not treat all applicants to TJ equally."[95]

Because "Asian-American applicants are disproportionately deprived of a level playing field," Hilton said, "It is clear that Asian-American students are disproportionately harmed by the Board's decision to overhaul TJ admissions."[96]

The school board cannot prove that it had a compelling interest in changing the racial makeup of TJ, said Hilton, because "racial balancing for its own sake is 'patently unconstitutional.'"[97]

Finally, Hilton noted, the school board could have increased the size of TJ or provided free test prep to applicants, rather than immediately defaulting to changing the admissions system to achieve "a particular racial outcome." "Since overhauling the process was not the last resort for the Board to accomplish its goals," he emphasized, "the Board's actions were not narrowly tailored."[98]

It was a huge victory for Nomani and her fellow parents whose rights were run over roughshod by the school board and county education officials.

Unfortunately, their victory was short-lived. The Fourth Circuit Court of Appeals issued a stay of Hilton's judgment, pending a hearing of the case on appeal. The U.S. Supreme Court refused to lift the stay. As of the writing of this book, the Fourth Circuit's hearing of the case has not yet occurred.

Nomani has continued her activism. She has sent Freedom of Information Act requests to around 200 school districts asking them for "the lists of consultants they hired for diversity, equity, inclusion, and anti-racism work, and then all the contracts related to those consultants." She was then able to find out the amounts of money spent and the programs that were funded.

She said, "I don't think parents understand the pyramid scheme that we've got going on with consultants that are part of numerous corporations registered under different names." "I ended up calling it the woke industrial complex," she observed.

Nomani understands the breadth and evil nature of CRT extremists. She says they are "a well-funded, well-organized network of activists, ideologues, and academics who are hell-bent on 'disrupting' education by infusing schools with their political ideological agendas."

"These activists," she observes, "are pitting students against each other by dividing them into categories of 'oppressed' and 'oppressor,' separating students based on race, creating a new hierarchy of human value that is bigoted, cruel, and racist."

Nomani says, "the idea of a hierarchy of human value is so dangerous and shame-based." "I was crushed under the weight of shame," she says, "and it is criminal when we have state-sanctioned shame."

"I have seen it," she warns, "in nations across the world," such as in Pakistan, "when religious schools would indoctrinate young boys with the idea of sectarianism and the shaming of others, like Hindus across the border, or Jews as less than them." "We see it everywhere and that is no way to live," she says, and "that's no value by which we can raise our children."

"We are in an existential struggle for the future of our country's children and the future of America," she warns.

Thankfully, she believes that parents have been activated and will be up to the challenge of defending the rights of their children. She explains that immigrant parents had to get over what had happened in their birth countries, but are now totally motivated to defend America and its values:

> The parents from China, they thought you could end up in jail. The parents from India thought the system is so corrupt, so why bother fighting? Everybody has seen injustice out there in the world. So I am really proud of these parents because I felt like they were people who chose America. These people chose America like my father did. They are fighting for the America they chose. So I hope everybody in America is inspired by the immigrants who are fighting for this nation.

She enthuses, "courage is contagious." "I really do believe," she reflects, "that with the example we had of parents, who overcame English as a second language, their own fears about citizenship, immigration status, and jobs, we inspired many other parents to stand up."

There are now hundreds of new activist parent groups across the country. "That's really profound," she says, because "there's a new generation of parents that are going to impact public policy."

"We must give parents not just the microphone," she entreats, "but a bullhorn." "This is a fight for America itself," she says, so "we all need to stand up and raise our voices."

CHAPTER 8

How Ethnic Studies Opens the Door to CRT: Elina Kaplan, Lia Rensin, and ACES

In California, a multi-year movement to proselytize ethnic studies through ideological lenses of critical consciousness and social justice has become a prominent vehicle of CRT's inroads into grade-level public education. Not only is the state-approved model curriculum endowed with the tenets of CRT, a more radical brand called Liberated Ethnic Studies is also being heavily marketed at the local level including California's largest school districts like the Los Angeles Unified School District and the San Diego Unified School District. It is safe to say that the K-12 ethnic studies movement is being hijacked by CRT.

Many citizens groups throughout California emerged to expose and combat the ideological hijacking of ethnic studies. Some, like the AMCHA Initiative, a non-profit group dedicated to documenting and reporting anti-semitism on college campuses, have raised concerns on existing ethnic studies models' anti-semitic nature. For instance, the AMCHA Initiative led a coalition of 74 organizations and thousands of individual petitioners to urge Gov. Newsom to veto the state bill that mandates ethnic studies in high schools.[99] They argued that the liberated curriculum would "marginalize Jewish students and fuel hatred and discrimination against the Jewish community." Other groups, including the Alliance for Constructive Ethnic Studies, Educators for Quality and Equality and Californians for Equal Rights Foundation, have taken the approach to fight the broader political connotations of teaching ethnic studies from a CRT perspective.

The Alliance for Constructive Ethnic Studies (ACES) is one among the most active opponents to Critical or Liberated Ethnic Studies. The group, which encompasses members of all racial backgrounds and political beliefs, was formed shortly after the state Department of Education unveiled California's first field draft of the Ethnic Studies Model Curriculum (ESMC), a bigoted and seriously flawed version rejected by both the California Legislature and Gov. Newsom.[100]

Although the political and education establishments brand the opposition as "bad-faith actors" committed to perpetuating "white supremacy,"[101] leaders and members of ACES are not a politically or racially homogeneous group.

To better understand their battles to reclaim ethnic studies from political indoctrination, we sat down with two cofounders of ACES – Elina Kaplan, a Jewish immigrant from the former Soviet Union who is a life-long Democrat and Lia Rensin, a Florida native of Jewish descent who leans conservative. These two unlikely allies, along with other cofounders of the grassroots organization, have teamed up in the wake of a statewide campaign in California to pioneer ethnic studies in K-12 classrooms.

ACES's motivation to save ethnic studies is about returning the discipline to its rightful and legislatively codified origin of "preparing pupils to be global citizens with an appreciation for the contributions of multiple cultures." There are stark differences between Liberated Ethnic Studies and Constructive

Ethnic Studies, almost two opposites of a discipline that "goes back to the 1960s," with the rise of the Third World Liberation Front in San Francisco. The student-led movement embraced a particular Neo-Marxist ideology that combined Leninism, Marxism and Maoism and also sported "a very strong anti-semitic streak." Over time, one branch of ethnic studies became more radicalized with an ideological agenda, promoted, politicized and often hijacked by so-called scholar-activists.

In Constructive Ethnic Studies, you have an emphasis on building bridges of understanding and empathy connecting people, and an emphasis on ethnic group accomplishments and contributions. Constructive Ethnic Studies doesn't shy away from talking about racism or oppression. But the emphasis is on what can be done, and how can students - how can people - come together to tackle these different issues. Open inquiry, multiple approaches to confronting racism, bigotry and other challenges that the society has are also emphasized. But, in the liberated or critical approach, the emphasis is on that oppressor victim paradigm. Militant resistance is a means of social change, along with dismantling the entire system. That often, if not, favors, then certainly excuses violence. The emphasis is on a specific ideology, particularly neo-Marxism and the entire movement to challenge imperialistic/colonial hegemonic beliefs and practices. Marxism and Marxist figures now are lionized and glorified without any acknowledgement of the oppression that came from them. Dismissing civil rights leaders such as Martin Luther King as "passive" and "docile" is also what we see in Liberated Ethnic Studies. In the chapter on "role models of color" in the first draft of the state model, out of

154 role models, figures like Martin Luther King, John Lewis, Thurgood Marshall are not listed.

A series of activist initiatives have been propagating critical pedagogy, a neo-Marxist educational principle, through ethnic studies at the K-12 level. ACES has worked hard to push back against Critical/Liberated Ethnic Studies through shining a light on the pedagogical and ideological issues in this approach, because ACES's founders are convinced that "if the vast majority of Americans knew what was actually behind this and knew what was being taught to kids in this discipline, they would absolutely favor Constructive Ethnic Studies."

At the state level, their awareness campaign and alliance building efforts have achieved some success in prompting the state to remove the most problematic contents from the finalized state model. For instance, references to a group of neo-Marxists and Black Panther revolutionary socialists such as Angela Davis, Assata Shakur, Bell Hooks, Fred Hampton, Mumia Abu-Jamal in the third field review of the model curriculum[102] were removed. In doing so, they helped moderate "the most controversial curriculum that has ever come out in the state of California." "We advocated and succeeded in removing an entire chapter on 154 significant figures that are people of color, including a unit on African-American role models that included this horrendous list of militant, Neo-Marxist figures," said Kaplan.

ACES also partnered up with other like-minded groups throughout California to lobby the State Legislature to introduce meaningful guardrails into AB 101, the state mandate for ethnic studies in every public high school. These guardrails are also touted by Gov. Newsom to "ensure that [ethnic studies] courses will be free from bias or bigotry and appropriate for all students."[103] As a result, the state has specific requirements for ethnic studies courses to:

1) Be "appropriate for use" with students "of all races, religions, nationalities, genders,

sexual orientations, and diverse ethnic and cultural backgrounds";

2) Not "reflect or promote, directly or indirectly, any bias, bigotry, or discrimination against any person or group of persons" within a protected group; and

3) "Not teach or promote religious doctrine."[104]

Additionally, AB101 guardrails highlight the vital role of local control and public consent: any local governing body that develops its own ethnic studies course must present it at a public meeting of the governing board, and shall not be approved until a subsequent public meeting at which the public has a chance to express its views on the proposed course.

ACES's advocacy work resulted in some positive changes in terms of content moderation in the state-approved model curriculum, voter education and also in light of their opponents' reactionary responses. "Even with relatively minor edits in the state model, the group that did the first draft was so offended by changes such as replacing the word 'capitalism' with 'exploitative economic systems,' that they dissociated themselves from the state curriculum to start our own thing," Kaplan recalled.

At the local level, where Liberated Ethnic Studies "has made significant inroads" in multiple school districts, ACES has focused on voter education and local organizing to share its findings and analyses with school board members, district leaders and parents. In Santa Clara County where Rensin lives, she led a public pressure campaign in which more than 500 local residents signed an open letter to the school board and superintendent to protest the schools' teaching of white supremacy as an explanatory factor behind "capitalism, land-ownership and religion." Consequently, the teaching module was removed. She also arranged expert witnesses and public speakers to attend two school board meetings to voice concerns about CRT.

Curricular materials also referred to the boycott, divestment, sanctions (BDS) movement against Israel as a positive social movement, along with praise for Black Lives Matter. The first model in California even called the foundation of the State of Israel, "as the Nakba, which means catastrophe," and featured a poem demonizing Jewish control of the media. For Rensin, "Some sample lessons adopt rhetoric that is blatantly anti-semitic, pro-BDS, anti-American, anti-establishment, anti-police rhetoric."

Notably, teaching ethnic studies in a critical, victim-vs-oppressor model is anti-semitic in nature because of a "confluence of economic success with oppressor status." "Jews tend to be seen as the top of that privilege hierarchy and the State of Israel as the oppressor, while the Palestinians as the victims," commented Kaplan. The Middle East conflict was the only international conflict addressed in previous ESMCs. Amplifying the anti-semitic foundation of Critical/Liberate Ethnic Studies is the discussion of Israeli "colonization" of Palestine as the basis of racism, which ignores the historical fact of centuries of oppression suffered collectively by the Jewish people.

Grounding her discussion of anti-semitism in the history of World War II when the German Nazi regime systematically targeted and murdered European Jews, Kaplan argues that "Critical Liberated Ethnic Studies is the number one threat to American Jews today, targeting an entire generation for this particular version of hatred that we've actually lived before."

More broadly, the movement in California to popularize Critical/Liberated Ethnic Studies, the prevalent mode of instruction for ethnic studies, is steeped in Marxism and neo-Marxist schools of thoughts. Ideological underpinnings of "youth activism, transformative resistance, and military resistance" facilitate the movement's ultimate goal to indoctrinate American kids. The oppressor-vs-victim ideological notion in Critical/Liberated Ethnic Studies has far-reaching, pedagogical ramifications as the principles of ethnic studies are infused into other K-12 disciplines such as math. Kaplan observed:

> The equitable math or ethno-mathematics is a combination of ethnic studies and math, which popularizes the idea that math is racist, the idea that Western math is racist, that teachers shouldn't insist on the right answer, and that you shouldn't use money. So, you see capitalism as the boogeyman in Liberated Ethnic Studies and it is often stated as the core basis of the injustice and the oppression that we have in society. It follows that the entire system has been completely broken down in order to change the oppressive nature of it.

Rensin recalled getting involved in the fight through her synagogue even though she is "not generally political in nature." She explained her concerns with indoctrination as a natural outcome of CRT-rooted ethnic studies: "Critical or Liberated Ethnic Studies has predetermined outcomes. They're not teaching kids to think critically."

Ironically, while CRT ideologues elevate "lived experiences" as the relativist dogma undergirding their divisive agendas including Critical/Liberated Ethnic Studies, they conveniently ignore those whose personal stories do not support the narrative of victimhood or white supremacy.

As for Kaplan, her background involved leaving the communist regime of the former Soviet Union in the territory of Belarus at the tender age of 11 when school-system indoctrination had begun back home. She remembers being proud when "the Neo-Marxist, Leninist indoctrination lessons" began in her fourth-grade classes, "a sign that you're becoming a real member of the society." Indoctrination carries through the entire educational system, as she also recalled a story in which her parents' friend "couldn't get a PhD in mathematics because he wasn't able to pass the Leninist class in graduate school."

To her dismay, the history of ideological capture is repeating itself in California through the institution of ethnic studies in the present time:

> I couldn't believe that I was seeing the same stuff that I was learning way back. In fact, one of the things that we find is that the people that came from communist countries like the former Soviet Union or Cuba, Venezuela or people that went through the Chinese Cultural Revolution are particularly horrified by this type of curriculum. Liberated Ethnic Studies was the same kind of flavor and had this fuzzy sense of the ideology that I had just started to learn in Soviet schools. There is this misguided emphasis on settler colonialism and imperialism as the roots of all evil. And growing out of this are genocide, God, religion, private property, white supremacy, patriarchy. The idea of private property and capitalism being equated with genocide and white supremacy is really quite stunning, obviously.

Marxism thoroughly informs the victim-oppressor model, the thematic thread of the entire model curriculum. Subsequently, CRT absorbs Marxist principles and simply replaces class struggles with race-based or ethnicity-based divisions. While none of the guiding principles in ESMC focuses on "contributions and accomplishments of ethnic groups," six out of the seven principles are obsessed with oppression, power structures, resistance and critique of empire building and white supremacy. Liberated/Critical Ethnic Studies also mentions the term "true democracy," a clear usage of Marxist language that equates to "the abolition of private property."

As a daughter of a German immigrant of Jewish descent, Rensin embraces America as the melting pot of different ethnicities and ideas. With her maternal grandparents having survived the Holocaust from a concentration camp, she appreciates her Jewish roots and sees the erasure of the history of Holocaust in Liberated Ethnic Studies as an egregious flaw flowing from Marxism and Neo-Marxism.

Moreover, having grown up in Rhode Island in the 1980s surrounded with friends and classmates from local Italian, Thai and Irish communities, Lia also learned to appreciate the natural diversity in America. So, when she first saw the Liberated Ethnic Studies curriculum, she immediately saw through "its attacks on some fundamental American values along with the shutting down of free speech and different viewpoints."

Their different upbringings have also led Kaplan and Rensin into two different directions in terms of politics. The former is a longtime registered Democrat and considers herself center left. She is alarmed by tides of increasing extremism on the far left and on the far right. Kaplan and other center-left members of ACES are particularly concerned about CRT's implementation as a lens in K-12 as "a manifestation of far-left extremism." For them, "placing students into oppressor and victim boxes is fundamentally incompatible with the liberal experiment for two reasons:"

> Firstly, it is important to teach students of all ages that life is gray, with positives and negatives. Some historical developments, of course, are purely negative, such as slavery. But dividing people into either oppressor or victim is fundamentally wrong: not only is it a problem to the liberal experiment, it is but also incompatible with any kind of reasonable education or reasonable pedagogy in a democratic society. Secondly, on a more micro level, I think it is a problem to teach any student that he or she is a part of an oppressor group or a part of the victim group. We have spoken with plenty of parents of color who

have problems with the notion of their kids being treated as perpetual victims.

Coming from a conservative political orientation as a life-long Republican, much to her family's chagrin, Rensin professes her fundamental belief in the American dream, the U.S. Constitution, and the equal opportunity and equal access principles. Recognizing our nation's evolving history and imperfect realities, she has been involved in volunteer organizations. "If you ignore what happened in the past and don't discuss every part of it, you're destined to repeat it."

For Rensin, "whitewashing history" is a big issue in Liberated/Critical Ethnic Studies. Applying a singular lens or telling one side of the story means that "kids are not learning that there are nuances to everything." She deems this approach illiberal: "How do we expect the next generation of leaders to be any better than the gridlock in Washington, DC if we don't teach them how to talk to each other, how to compromise and how to appreciate differences as opposed to demonizing them?" Judging someone solely on the basis of the color of their skin or by virtue of their political persuasion is a huge disservice to our country.

Liberated/Critical Ethnic Studies presents a totalitarian threat to liberal democracy by promoting the notion of systemic racism and hatred toward American exceptionalism. The intended goal is to incite left-ward youth activism and legitimize a complete rewrite of our institutions and systems through "transformative resistance." The result will be disastrous because kids are ideologically captured to demonize the United States on one hand and glorify brutal regimes in other parts of the world in the name of ethnic diversity. "Our kids will lose perspective of what is reality and what is not. If we are so horrible and people didn't have an opportunity to better their lives here, they would not have chosen to come here in the first place.

While they come from vastly different backgrounds, Kaplan and Rensin share a common goal of saving public education by way of rescuing ethnic studies. For Kaplan, "it's nothing short of dictating how the next generation is going to interact with each other or of what is driving the nature of our society." For Rensin, this is a fight of a lifetime:

> What we're seeing in today's society is cancel culture and not being able to have a dialogue with anyone who doesn't agree with you or automatically like the victim/oppressor thing. You either agree with me or you're evil. The resistance has to come from people who are aware of what's going on, who push back and say you as educators are supposed to be educating my kids, you're not supposed to be indoctrinating my kids. Our kids shouldn't learn that . . . rioting or destroying property or skipping classes or doing all those things. That's not the right way to affect change. And if ethnic studies is supposed to be about effecting positive change, then it should be done in a positive way.

ACES has adopted a nonpartisan approach. Kaplan further stresses the importance of alliance building: "Fundamentally, this liberal or critical approach is a problem for every group, whether they fall on the side of the oppressor or the victim in this ridiculous paradigm."

Ideally, ethnic studies, a controversial topic that is facing several legal challenges, should not be taught through any particular ideological lens without introducing counter-balancing perspectives. An equity lens must be discussed alongside an equality lens. A race-conscious, anti-racism perspective should be analyzed in relation to a race-blind perspective of constitutional equality, without any particular bias or tilt toward one view over the other.

The legal definition according to AB2016 is that ethnic studies is an interdisciplinary study of different ethnicities and cultures throughout the United States to prepare students to be global citizens with an appreciation for the contributions of multiple cultures. Most sensible citizens, across the political aisle, support a positive approach and agree with the non-negotiable importance of teaching cultures, history, and racism in our K-12 classrooms so that our students become informed citizens with cross-cultural understanding.

Most individuals, once sufficiently equipped with knowledge of the thematic principles of ethnic studies versus its ideologically motivated implementation in practice, should also be wary of CRT's role in Liberated/Critical Ethnic Studies. By all accounts, the latter's obsession with power and oppression, crudely divided by race or ethnicity, shows its substantial departure from the legally required focus on contributions and unity.

In summary, the ongoing debate surrounding ethnic studies is not whether or not an educational entity should teach ethnic studies. This has long been settled among common-sense education experts, educators and community members. The big thorny question is how a public education institution should teach the discipline. Should ethnic studies be taught to highlight tribulations, perseverance and contributions or to accentuate intra-group struggles, power imbalances and victimhood? Should it be a stand-alone course for high school students or should it be infused as a pedagogical approach into various other disciplines across different grades? To what extent should CRT inform the teaching of cultures and ethnicities? ACES's advocacy and awareness building work has enriched the real debate and informed the public about the interlocking complexity of the issue.

Kaplan and Rensin understand that the finalized state model curriculum still has an unbalanced framework with politically charged guiding principles, and that the state rejected Liberated/Critical Ethnic Studies is aggressively invading local school districts including Los Angeles Unified School District, Castro Valley Unified School District, Hayward Unified School District and others.

"There is a long way to go," said Kaplan.

CHAPTER 9

Forcing Schools to Be Transparent: Nicole Solas and Kelly Schenkoske

Historically, education has always been viewed as the responsibility of the parents. But in recent years, more schools than ever are working to keep parents out of the classroom – whether through prohibiting classroom visits, discouraging school tours, or preventing access to curriculum materials.

Due to the pandemic, that power struggle began to shift. Every household had a window into their child's classroom. Online learning necessitated by the pandemic enabled parents to finally answer for themselves: what is my child learning in school? It was through the computer lens that many families, for the first time, learned how some American classrooms had begun touting divisive critical race theory propaganda.

Nicole Solas

A recent national survey[105] found that 84 percent of Americans believe that parents should be able to see all educational materials and curriculum plans used in their child's classroom. Despite the public's overwhelming support, one shocking story of a Rhode Island mother demonstrates the length to which some schools go to shut parents out.

This is the story of Nicole Solas, a Rhode Island mom who received a threat of a lawsuit from her local school district. The supposed offense? She asked too many questions about her daughter's education.

In 2021, she went to enroll her kindergartener in a South Kingston, Rhode Island public school. Before beginning the school year, she first requested a tour. To her surprise, the request was denied. She went forward with enrolling her daughter but explained, "that felt very unnatural for me to just drop my kid off somewhere and not know what's going on."

She had hoped that the tour would help her get a better idea of what her child's experience would be but, "they wanted me to drop my daughter off at school, never seeing the inside of the school, never meeting a single teacher, and never knowing anything about what she would learn."

Her unease with what her daughter was potentially learning was not unwarranted. Before her daughter was old enough to begin school, the district sent out an email in the summer of 2020. She recalled, "it was a very radical political message that was sent out to the whole community saying, 'we need to become anti-racist, we need to employ radical empathy.' It was all this highly politicized language. And I thought it was really bizarre coming out of the school district."

The term *anti-racist* is a political term that comes from author Ibram X. Kendi, who runs the Anti-racist Research and Policy Center at American University. In his book, *How to Be Anti-racist*, he writes,

> The black body is instructed to become an American body. The American body is the white body. The black body strives to assimilate into the American body. The American body rejects the black body. The

black body separates from the American body. The black body is instructed to assimilate into the American body – and history and consciousness duel anew.

But there is a way to get free. To be anti-racist is to emancipate oneself from the dueling consciousness. To be anti-racist is to conquer the assimilationist consciousness and the segregationist consciousness. The white body no longer presents itself as the American body; the black body no longer strives to be the American body, knowing there is no such thing as the American body, only American bodies, racialized by power.[106]

She had hoped that the tour would quell her concern that the school employed such radical, political teachings. Since no tour was offered, she started asking the teachers questions about the curriculum.

The teachers responded by lending her a textbook that they claimed outlined their curriculum. But when Nicole asked a teacher friend in the district about it, she said that the textbook was outdated and no longer used.

So, she pivoted and decided to call the school's principal to address her unanswered questions.

Among her questions, she wanted to know whether the district planned to follow through with anti-racism teachings. At this, the principal went quiet for a long time, and she perceived the principal felt nervous to answer.

Eventually, the principal affirmed that the school did teach anti-racism and critical race theory. She then provided an example of how they teach this line of thinking in kindergarten. During November lessons, the teacher would ask the kindergarteners, "what could have been done differently on Thanksgiving?"

She remarked, "it's an absurd question. It's actually a politically loaded question." She's right. The question would go over the head of kindergarteners, merely working as an introduction to the idea that something should have been done differently. When she pressed the principal to ask for the pedagogy to back up the Thanksgiving question, the principal said that she did not have any idea.

The principal then cut the conversation short and encouraged her to file public records requests to get her questions answered.

Before filing public records requests, she also sent about 20 or 25 questions regarding anti-racist teachings and gender theory lessons to the school, to see if she could get her questions answered. Again, in the email, she was directed to the public records request process.

She suspected that the school hoped that requiring a formal public records request, which is potentially costly and time-consuming, would dissuade her from pursuing answers to her questions. But she remained undeterred.

Public record requests encourage government transparency and accountability, vital principles for a healthy democracy. Public records requests were legally formalized in 1966 when President Lyndon Johnson signed the Freedom of Information Act in response to the previous administration's refusal to share documents regarding the dismissal of thousands of federal workers accused of being communists.

Following the Freedom of Information Act, states began to adopt their own public records laws. According to Rhode Island state law, if the requested document is twenty or fewer pages, no copying fee will be charged. Otherwise, it costs $.15 for each page. Additionally, the entity (in her case, the school board) can charge $15 an hour for the time necessary to retrieve the requested documents. These costs could discourage the average filer.

But with a law degree from Roger Williams University and having practiced law for several years before becoming a mother, Solas knew how to efficiently make public records requests.

Over the course of several weeks, she filed approximately 160 similar requests.

After weeks of largely pleasant exchanges with district staff over her public records requests, suddenly everything changed. she learned of an upcoming school board meeting agenda item, "filing lawsuit against Nicole Solas."[107]

The school district apparently planned to sue her for doing the very thing repeatedly requested of her: filing public records requests.

"That was a huge surprise to me! Definitely a shock. I had never even been to a school board meeting ever before. And now my name was on it," she said.

In the nearly four-hour-long meeting, only six minutes were used to discuss another agenda item. The rest of the time was devoted entirely to discussing whether to sue her for asking too many questions.

The portion on Solas began with a written statement by a school member who said, "this issue is a much larger one. One that involves a disturbing attempt by a national organized racist group to create chaos and intimidate our district as we discuss bringing equity and anti-racism curriculum to our schools." The statement earned a series of boos and laughter from the large audience.

The opening statement revealed what the lawsuit threat was truly about: the school district feared that if the community saw the content of the curriculum she requested, they would not be able to covertly adopt the controversial critical race theory curriculum.

She summarized the school district's motivations best, "my school committee talked about my suspected political motivations, my moral character. They were really looking to ostracize me from society and destroy my life because I had just started participating in my community since I was going to enroll my daughter in school. And this was really their way of letting everyone know that if you asked too many questions, they were going to attack you."

Not only did the district imply Solas was a racist and extremist, but the school board claimed she did not have a child in the district. This was not true.

As noted by the public records act specialist during the meeting, for every public records request that goes unanswered, the district could be subjected to a fine of up to $75,000.

Furthermore, the board claimed that expending the hours necessary to answer the public records requests would be a waste of taxpayer money and would distract administrators from focusing on more important tasks. Thus, the board reasoned, since the fines would cost too much and since the department didn't want to invest the time necessary to be transparent with the curriculum, apparently the only other option was to sue Solas.

Not all school board members felt comfortable with threatening to sue her. One commented that although she felt her actions were a "political ploy" that "at the same time unintentionally chills progress or chills parents' access to information." Although the board member misinterpreted her actions, she still recognized that obstructing transparency and threatening parents violates ethics.

Another board member suggested just posting all the curriculum online to appease her. The expert on public records requests confirmed that in another school district she had worked in, that tact helped not only parents but teachers, too.

In response, another school board member asked, "are we allowed to be speaking about curriculum right now?" At this, the audience laughed, and the subject changed.

As it turned out, the school board was in the middle of a curriculum audit. Long before she filed her public records requests, the district had been cited for not having a codified curriculum. Clearly, the district wanted to avoid showing that they were in violation of state education standards.

Many had come out in support of Nicole. Others wanted to speak in support of critical race theory. Nicole spoke first. Her comments deserve to be quoted in full.

> I think we all know my name. It's on the agenda.
> And I'm not stating my address, we all know
> why not. I am a mother with a child enrolled

in the district going into kindergarten. I had questions about her education and you didn't answer them. You told me to submit public record requests to answer my questions. I did what you told me. And now you're holding a public meeting to discuss suing me for doing what you told me to do.

This meeting was meant to publicly humiliate me, and it didn't work. I want to talk about the statement you issued today. It was replete with critical race verbiage such as equity which raises serious concerns about CRT in the district. Equity is a CRT code word for discrimination based on race. The school committee should focus on equality in treating students without regard to race. Why is the school committee so obsessed with treating students based on their skin color? We need answers to that, not lawsuits against parents. Thank you.[108]

As explained earlier, equity departs drastically from the tra ditional understanding of equality. Equality champions equal opportunities, or equal means to the end. However, equity advocates for identical outcomes, or identical ends to the means.

Ironically, it is precisely because of mankind's inherent diversity that makes identical outcomes impossible. All human beings have unique talents and natural proclivities and thus something individually valuable to contribute to society.

Critical race theory takes the concept of equity and uses it to justify pitting individuals against one another on the basis of race. Thus, her concern that the district's use of the word equity in the school board statement could demonstrate the presence of critical race theory curriculum in the schools is not unfounded.

Following a two hour public hearing, including comments by supportive parents and others allegedly asked by the school committee to speak against Solas, the school board after lengthy deliberations voted for a new amendment to pursue mediation rather than a lawsuit. Ultimately, the school district decided not to sue Solas. Of the decision, she said, "it is still unclear what they would sue me for. Perhaps an injunction on public records requests, but that would be unconstitutional."

But after the school board meeting, the local teachers' union sent a constable to Nicole's door with a complaint. Receiving the complaint "astounded" Solas because she was not sure what legal basis the union even had to sue her.

When special interest groups such as a union sue private individuals without legal basis, often the end game is to drain defendants with legal fees, to intimidate them with bankruptcy.

But the union knew, that at that time, she was already represented by the Goldwater Institute, a non-profit which offers free representation to individuals facing constitutional issues in court. Thus, filing a lawsuit against her could neither intimidate nor financially harm her.

The union's complaint alleged that she could not receive curricula because being transparent would potentially subject teachers to harassment from national conservative groups. Again, that is an unconstitutional claim – you cannot interfere with someone's civil right to get public information.

Of course, no one wants anyone to be harassed. But as she said, "if anyone's being harassed here, it's me, by, you know, this teacher's union with $300 million dollars in institutional power."

Rhode Island Supreme Court case law states that a third party (such as a teachers' union) cannot interfere with a public records request process. Thus, the teacher union's case had another major issue: just filing the case itself is evidence against them.

In response, the Goldwater Institute filed a counterclaim on behalf of Solas against the union in August 2021.

As of this writing, the judge's decision in the case is still forthcoming.

Most parents agree that kids should be taught *how* to think, not *what* to think. But before getting to that point, parents must know what their child's education looks like.

Ultimately, Solas believes that curriculum change is a fight that will be won in the courts. Legal precedent must be established to rule political indoctrination in school as unconstitutional.

Inspired by her story, Goldwater advocated legislation in their home state of Arizona requiring schools to post learning materials online, which was enacted in March 2022. The legislation gives parents an informed idea of what goes on in the classroom.

Just two weeks later, Florida followed Arizona's example to require transparency, allow parental review of materials, and set curriculum standards.

A *Washington Post* article stated that at least 15 other states are considering similar legislation as of March 2022.[109]

As a result of her experience, Solas thought a lot about the meaning and purpose of education in the public square. She remarked, "it's unfair to impose any political indoctrination on kids because it actually takes away their ability to take knowledge in its purest form, and then have their own ideas what that knowledge means to them and in their life, and how that is going to shape their view of the world."

When she asked her daughter's kindergarten teacher a simple question – what will be taught this year - she never expected what unfolded next.

Perhaps her dedication can be best understood as a mother's protective instinct for her child. When asked why she endeavors, she expressed, "this toxic ideology could just destroy a little child's soul, right? For me, this is a spiritual battle."

Kelly Schenkoske

Moms, dads, and everyday folk have worked tirelessly to combat the ideological takeover of our nation's K-12 schools and they are the true heroes of this new movement. Kelly Schenkoske is a shining example of this emerging force.

A California native born and raised in the Monterey Bay area, she comes from a family that epitomizes America's natural ethnic diversity: on her mother's side, she descends from Italian, British, Irish and French heritage, while her paternal heritage is a combination of Mexican, Sicilian, Polish and African. "I am a blend of many – I am an American," she says.

Growing up in the town of Pacific Grove, she attended the Pacific Grove Unified School District from kindergarten through the end of high school in the 1990s and 2000s. Her experience in public schools was largely positive, helping shape her philosophy of education that "young people should be given the opportunity to love learning, achieve academic excellence through merit, and also be inspired to grow in all subjects."

With trust in the local public-school system to challenge students in academics and value them as individuals, Schenkoske and her husband, whom she met in high school, sent their two children to the same school district.

As a stay-at-home mom, she tried to engage with the schools and teachers proactively through volunteering as a classroom parent, a library assistant, and at the Parent Teacher Association. But to her great disappointment, the experience she had there as a parent was much different from her student days.

Schenkoske started to notice "a push for agendas on one political side," biased portrayals with a leftward slant, and vilification of Judeo-Christian values. She recalled the school district music teacher's attempt to rewrite all traditional Christmas carols, such as "Come all ye faithful."

Her sneaky suspicion of indoctrination turned into a real struggle at the end of 2018 when she shared her concerns regarding the implementation of the California Healthy Youth Act with school officials and fellow parents.

She spoke at several school board meetings, informed other parents through social media, and gave media interviews. Others had turned to her to represent concerned parents who feared retaliation from the school district.

Shortly after giving her public comment at the school board meeting, she started receiving hate messages and online harassment. A conversation thread was started in a local Facebook group to condemn her activism. Some in the thread called for violence against her and her family.

By mid-2019, she no longer felt safe sending her children back to school, even after she had filed a police report. So, she and her husband decided to homeschool their two kids.

However, pulling her kids out of public school did not mean an end of her education advocacy work. She wanted to continue to inform the community and fellow parents with accurate and complete information.

One thing that has stood out for her in her research of major developments or trends in public education is the interconnectedness among "comprehensive sex education, ethnic studies, DEI initiatives and CRT."

With the help of an attorney family friend, she submitted multiple public records requests to the Monterey County Office of Education, Salinas Union High School District, Pacific Grove Unified School District, and Spreckels Union School District.

What she uncovered is an extensive trail of political indoctrination. For instance, she acquired a 571-page document describing the implementation of ethnic studies in the Salinas Union High School District. "Critical race theory" appears 44 times in the document. The U.S. Department of Education is also mentioned in the document as a reference in favor of teaching CRT in K-12.

She also stumbled upon a teaching chart called "The Matrix of Social Identity and Intersectional Power."

The chart lists a myriad of racial categories, gender identities, gender expressions, forms of discrimination/oppression in layers of intersectional identities that make up "who we are." Such balkanization, predicated on the conceptual inventions of power, oppression and privilege, should have no place in a K-12 classroom.

Like many other school districts in California, Salinas Union High has adopted Critical Ethnic Studies, which has been described earlier in this book.

Equipped with concrete evidence of CRT hijacking local schools, she spoke passionately about it at a Salinas Union High School District board meeting in late 2021:

> You are also including a chant [in the curriculum] to Black Lives Matter and a unity chant [to Aztec and Mayan deities]. Since when did public education become a political activist organization?[110]

Many source documents and teaching examples she identified also have linkages to the LatCrit (Latina & Latino Critical Legal Theory) framework, a sub-genre of CRT intended to:

> (1) to develop a critical, activist, and inter-disciplinary discourse on law and society affecting Latinas/os/x, and (2) to foster both the development of coalitional theory and practice as well as the accessibility of this knowledge to agents of social and legal transformative change.[111]

Schenkoske sees through the deception and lies of indoctrination as "adult ideological manipulation" masquerading as "student agency." "It is really the adults who are the puppet masters behind the student."

Such manipulation is certainly ironic as the ideologues and teacher-activists are imposing political dogmas in an oppressive way while encouraging students to "dismantle oppressive power structures." She says that the cost is hefty:

> We're seeing students being leveraged towards political activism, while at the same time being robbed of the opportunity to advance

academically and robbed of the opportunity to have a childhood.

She is right. "Ultimately, that systemic change goes against everything we've valued, that includes family, community and individuality." Everyone loses.

She continues to keep track of new developments in local areas, including the intricate network among local schools, state agencies, and higher education institutions that promote a race-based ideological agenda, educates parents, hosts a podcast, organizes grassroots events and speaks out at school board meetings and community gatherings.

When she meets with local residents, she hands out brochures and pamphlets on SEL, CRT and CSE. She even keeps textbooks and full curricular documents on these topics in her car just in case others would listen to her quick pitches. "Once they find out about what is really going on, people are rightfully shocked."

She expressed her optimism for the eventual victory of the anti-CRT movement and her encouragement for others with similar concerns about public education:

> Each person has a group, a circle of friends and acquaintances that they know and people that they interact with in their communities. Getting out there is key and speaking up right now is absolutely necessary. Don't be surprised when any voice that doesn't conform to the agenda in a school district is met with a calculated and organized response aimed at silencing dissenting voices. Do not let that stop you from speaking up boldly and courageously.

CHAPTER 10

Confronting CRT, Courage on the School Board: Emily Ortiz-Wichmann and Mari Barke

With all the controversy over race-based indoctrination in the classroom, school boards have become the focal point of community concern.

"It will be up to parents to watch closely what their children are being taught and to petition their school board when schools cross the line between education and indoctrination," observed Max Eden, a senior fellow at the Manhattan Institute.[112] Parents have indeed mobilized and some school boards have responded.

From liberal Washington state to conservative Georgia, school boards have passed resolutions banning critical race theory in classroom instruction and in training for school employees.[113]

As school boards have taken center stage in the debates over CRT, the public is now focused more than ever on who board members are.

Emily Ortiz-Wichmann

Emily Ortiz-Wichmann was until recently a longtime member of the Oceanside, California school board. Her mother was an immigrant from Mexico who was a descendant of an indigenous tribe. Her father, who was also of Mexican heritage, had a third-grade education but later became successful through hard work, owning three homes and travelled the world – values that influenced Ortiz-Wichmann.

Speaking about her father, she said, "he didn't know how to write," so, "he always made me do paperwork for him."

Yet, her father believed in the American dream. "He wanted money in the bank, he wanted his own home, and he wanted to travel the world," she recalled. Her father ended up doing well in life, owning three homes, and traveling from Egypt to China.

She said, "he did that with hard work." Her father's experience highly influenced her. She tells children to follow her father's example "and not look for excuses, not look for victims."

"My philosophy on education is simple," she says. "I feel it should provide the opportunity for every student to learn to the best of his or her ability and to teach them the basic academics, such as reading, writing, science, and also critical thinking skills."

She also points to Dr. Martin Luther King, Jr. Growing up, she heard him say that what mattered was the content of a person's character, not the color of a person's skin.

"I was a young adult when he said that," she remembered, "and being a Mexican or Latino, even though I felt good about myself, I looked around and not everybody thought that." However, after Dr. King uttered those famous words, she thought, "Yeah, it's about me, not about my race, not my color."

Her community of Oceanside is a racially diverse city north of San Diego. She says, "As parents, we felt the camaraderie of people who were different colors, different races, different ethnicities."

"I love my community," she says, and "our kids are precious." It was because of her love for Oceanside and for the city's children that she ran for and was elected to the local school board.

She says that the advent of divisive teaching techniques such as CRT have caused a great deal of concern for the Hispanic community:

> Our people are humble. They're working. They want to send their kids off to school, and they just need to work. They don't have time for meetings. Some of them don't understand how they can even speak out. I have several people that will talk to me, some are first generation or not legal, and they're appalled at what's going on.

When she sees CRT-influenced instruction putting children into categories of oppressor or oppressed based on race, she says, "we're challenging that." She points out, "My husband is White, so my kids are half and half." She asks, "So what do I tell my half-and-half kids, my White kid?" "Do I tell them their father is an oppressor and I'm oppressed?"

To show how absurd race-based thinking can get, she said that a person on a committee on which she served told her that he believed that she felt the way she did "because you're lighter in color." She replied, "I went, what?"

She pointed out that in a 2021 slide presentation on "Equity and Cultural Proficiency in OUSD" put out by the Oceanside district, a top school official is quoted defining equity as "an intentional ability to give up privilege and power for a greater good." "In my experiences," she observed, such a definition "means communism."

The presentation also included a slide on professional learning focusing on "Unconscious and Implicit Bias Workshops" where staff would be taught about, among other things, "Power and Privilege" and "Unbiasing."

Also, anti-racism/equity/justice toolkits were given to school leaders. Further, educators were "trained in the Restorative practices model to address the intersection between bias, expectations, and student discipline."

Ortiz-Wichmann says, "Critical race theory is based on neo-Marxist theories of privilege," with an emphasis on "systemic racism, that's what it's all about."

William Galston, a senior fellow at the Brookings Institution and a former domestic policy advisor to President Bill Clinton, has pointed out[114], "Critical race theory is an explicitly left-wing movement inspired by the thinking of an Italian neo-Marxist, Antonio Gramsci."[115]

While classical Marxism focuses on economic classes, such as the bourgeoisie and the proletariat, Galston observed that Gramsci "focused on hegemony," which emphasizes societal arrangements in the existing order that are meant to keep down dominated classes.

Because CRT views current American societal arrangements as inherently oppressive to dominated racial classes, proponents reject the "work hard and get ahead" philosophy of Ortiz-Wichmann's father, despite the fact that it worked for him. As Galston has noted:

> *Critical race theory rejects the principle of equality of opportunity.* Its adherents insist that equality of opportunity is a myth, not a reality, in today's America, and that those who pursue it are misguided. The real goal is equality of results, measured by black share of income, wealth and social standing. Critical race theorists reject the idea that sought-after goods should be distributed through systems that evaluate and reward "merit."
>
> This metric is unacceptable . . . because certain "conceptions of merit function not as a neutral basis for distributing resources and opportunity, but rather as a repository of hid-

den, race-specific preferences for those who have the power to determine the meaning and consequences of 'merit.'" These critics don't specify which conceptions of merit, if any, they would find acceptable.[116]

Following Gramsci's neo-Marxist lead, Galston notes, "critical race theory has used mainstream concepts such as equality and inclusion to wage a highly effective war of position against liberal ideology."[117]

"But now," says Galston, "the debate has moved to states and school districts around the country, and many parents don't like what they are seeing."[118]

Indeed, Ortiz-Wichmann says that parents and children in her community do not like what they are seeing. "It's not what our kids need," she says, "and it's not Oceanside."

"If you go to our football games," she observes, "you see all different colors, from the blondest of blondes to Samoans with their lavalavas to Mexicans, and it's a beautiful mixture of our people in Oceanside."

"Our parents will embrace any child no matter what color," she says, because "they're all a part of us."

CRT is "just mixing them up," she warns, and "is detrimental to our kids, making them worry about who's doing them wrong instead of just buckling down and getting it done."

For Ortiz-Wichmann, "my gut tells me it's wrong" because "you don't treat people that way and you don't manipulate people that way."

Mari Barke

North on the I-405 freeway from Ortiz-Wichmann is another school board member who comes from a very different background, but who has also come to similar conclusions about CRT and the danger it poses to children.

Born in the town of Gardena, just south of Los Angeles International Airport, Mari Barke grew up selling blue jeans at swap meets with her father.

Her parents were divorced, but her father, who had only an eighth-grade education, pushed his children to go to college. Barke, who is Jewish, went to California State University Northridge. She graduated cum laude with a degree in finance.

She spent the first part of her career working in the insurance industry, where she ended up "managing about $30 million commercial territory of brokers."

After her first child was born, she decided to leave big-industry life and join the family store. "I spent the next 20 years in that store running it," she said.

Unfortunately, the store had to close in 2016 due to the changing retail climate, so she had to look for other things to do.

She was interested in politics and public policy, so she became involved with the California Policy Center (CPC), a conservative policy organization in Orange County as head of California Local Elected Officials, which is a CPC-sponsored organization.

Once in the policy world, people started to ask her to run for office. Having gone to public schools and having children, "I was asked to run for the Orange County Board of Education."

One of the key responsibilities of the county board is to act as a type of appeals court for approving charter schools, which are publicly funded schools that are independent of school districts and have more flexibility to innovate.

In California, local school district boards have initial approval authority over whether a charter school can be established. If the district board turns down a charter school's petition, then the charter organizers can appeal to the county board.

She had seen the award-winning film documentary *Waiting for Superman*, which told the stories of several children who were ill-served by regular public schools and who were trying to get into better-performing charter schools.

"I watched that movie," she said, and "I cried."

Her daughter was small in stature, and she was bullied in her regular public school, so she and her husband sent her to a private high school.

"There were a lot of children in Orange County and beyond that didn't have that luxury," she said, "so I thought it was time to give back and to provide the educational choices for everyone's children that my children enjoyed." She therefore decided to run for a spot on the county board.

She also understood the trials of disadvantaged parents and their children from her time teaching English as a second language (ESL). She had learned Spanish growing up and conversed with Spanish-speaking customers at the swap meet.

She met one little girl named Vanessa "who used to come with her grandma to class and I just adored her." Teaching ESL, she said, "was a great experience."

Mari proved to be a born candidate. She wore out shoe leather. "I walked 14,000 houses myself," she recalled.

Her face-to-face personal campaign paid off. Although she started out behind when the first votes came in on election night, she eventually pulled ahead and won.

Once elected, she pushed not only for greater school choice options, like charter schools, for her constituents, she also promoted greater transparency and community involvement. She got the board and the county education office to move board meetings to the evenings so more people could attend and got meetings live-streamed on YouTube so more people could view board proceedings.

Just as in other parts of the country, however, critical race theory and race-based classroom instruction flared up in Orange County.

In the Los Alamitos Unified School District, located in northern Orange County, a high-school science class and a middle-school English class had assigned an opinion article entitled, "Why I'm a Racist," written by a White New Jersey man and which was originally published in the *Huffington Post*.[119]

Many parents were upset that the schools had assigned the article, but the district dismissed their concerns as misinformation. Of course, such a haughty response did not satisfy the parents, so they turned to the Orange County Board of Education for help.

She and her board colleagues responded by organizing two forums in the summer of 2021 where experts would testify and where the public would be allowed to have input. These two expert forums, which focused on CRT and ethnic studies, were the first such events sponsored by an elected educational body in the country.

When she opened the first forum, she commented: "As an elected government body entrusted with the mission to offer leadership and resources for our 29 school districts and [Orange County Department of Education] schools, the Orange County Board of Education has a vested interest in making sure that all our trustees are sufficiently educated on these two interrelated topics, so that we can better inform the public and guide various schools in our county."[120]

It should be pointed out that according to the California School Boards Association's definition, "Critical race theory holds that racism is embedded in American systems and institutions and part of everyday life, so people can perpetuate and benefit from racism, through their normal, everyday existence, even if they do so unintentionally."[121]

So, while the CSBA claims that not all White people are racist, this acknowledgment means nothing in the world of critical race theory. In fact, it makes things worse because an individual White person may not be bigoted or prejudiced but will always benefit from an inherently racist American societal structure. Hence, White people will always be viewed as privileged beneficiaries of racist government and economic institutions regardless of their own individual circumstances, no matter how dire they may be.

Testifying at the forums were ten experts, including UCLA law professor Richard Sander, University of San Diego law professor Maimon Schwarzschild, California Baptist University assistant professor of intercultural studies Damon Horton, plus one of the co-authors of this book.

In his opening statement at the first forum, Professor Schwarzschild, who is the co-editor of the 2020 book *A Dubious Expediency*, which details the negative impact of race preferences in higher education, said that "Critical race theory or—quite misleadingly—'anti-racism'" claims "that America's institutions—including constitutional government, separation of powers, and the Bill of Rights—are camouflages for racial oppression."[122]

Schwarzschild made the important point that in classrooms where CRT-influenced curricula are used, "these ideas are not presented as one point of view, contested by other and very different ideas, facts, and interpretations, with pupils taught to think independently and to develop skills of critical thinking and the evaluation of evidence." Rather, he said:

> On the contrary, there is now widespread evidence that these curricula center on psychological techniques to "train" pupils that their race determines nearly everything about them. Pupils are separated by race for "Privilege Walks" and other classroom exercises, inculcating the idea that white pupils are privileged oppressors, and that non-white pupils are victims of this pervasive oppression. These lessons advance the claim that any counter-evidence or reasoned criticisms are themselves racist and a discredited defense of whiteness. Students who venture to object to being deemed privileged, and to being held personally responsible for white racism, are ridiculed for their "white fragility" and in effect are compelled to voice agreement as to their racial guilt.[123]

Recall the privilege walk that Joshua had to endure in his middle school. Also recall Gabs Clark's son William, who was not allowed to graduate by his school because he refused to go along with being labeled privileged because of his racial appearance.

Indeed, as in Gabs Clark's federal lawsuit against her son's school, Professor Schwarzschild laid out clear legal reasons why schools and school boards should refrain from imposing CRT indoctrination in their classrooms.

"The Constitution itself is held by the Supreme Court to forbid schools to coerce children to express agreement or adherence to any sentiment in violation of their conscience," he pointed out.[124]

In *West Virginia State Board of Education v. Barnette*, which involved a school forcing students to salute the American flag, the Court cited First Amendment freedom of speech and said, "If there is any fixed star in our constitutional constellation, it is that no official, high or petty, can prescribe what shall be orthodox in politics, nationalism, religion, or other matters of opinion or force citizens to confess by word or act their faith therein."[125]

No wonder then that the federal judge in Clark's case indicated that she and her son were likely to win on the merits of their arguments.

In addition, as noted in Clark's lawsuit, Schwarzschild observed that Title VI of the Civil Rights Act of 1964 "protects all students who attend schools receiving federal funding from being treated differently based on their actual or perceived race, color, or national origin."[126]

Further, Title VI is violated if there is racial harassment, which is defined as unwelcome conduct based on a pupil's race or national origin, and if that harassment is "severe or persistent enough to constitute a hostile or abusive educational environment."

Title VI notes, "young children are particularly impressionable, and that schools have a special obligation to provide a non-discriminatory environment conducive to learning."[127]

Also, given the highly ideological CRT-based professional development training given to teachers, with mounting examples of White teachers being accused of racism and forced to confront their privilege, Scwharzschild underscored, "Discrimination against employees on the basis of race, sex, and national origin is prohibited by Title VII of the Civil Rights Act of 1964 as amended, and harassment severe or pervasive enough to create a hostile work environment is held to be within the prohibitions of Title VII."[128]

The bottom line, he said, "There is potential for legal liability, in short, under these federal laws among others, and under state law as well, when public schools adopt racialist and racially abusive classroom techniques and curricula."[129]

Indeed, California's Education Code states: "A teacher shall not give instruction and a school district shall not sponsor any activity that promotes a discriminatory bias on the basis of race or ethnicity, gender, religion, disability, nationality, or sexual orientation."[130]

The forums were a huge success. As noted in a January 2022 board white paper on the forums, the two informational events "had an overwhelmingly positive reception among Orange County's diverse parents, grandparents, and community members, who came forth to give public comments in support of unity and in opposition to divisive indoctrination."[131]

An article published by the CSBA on the forums cited the comments of one member of the public who seemed to speak for many at the forums:

> I am a Japanese father. I believe ethnic studies and critical race theory promotes racism and hate. It focuses on our country's defeats rather than our victories. Today, anyone of any race can be successful in America with hard work and determination. I'm living proof of that.[132]

Interestingly, the CSBA tries to have it both ways when it comes to CRT. On the one hand, it says, "There is no evidence that CRT is widespread in K-12 education," but then admits, "There is no definitive resource documenting the prevalence of CRT in schools."[133]

CSBA tries to minimize the connection between CRT and California's model ethnic studies curriculum, but then admits, "the model curriculum recommends that teachers and administrators should familiarize themselves with current scholarly research around ethnic studies, such as critically and culturally/community relevant and responsive pedagogies, critical race theory, and intersectionality, which are key theoretical frameworks and pedagogies that can be used in ethnic studies research and instruction."[134]

The model ethnic studies curriculum also defines CRT as arguing that "racism is embedded within systems and institutions that replicate racial inequality—codified in law, embedded in structures, and woven into public policy." In other words, CRT says that racism is inherent in American society, and that is the framework and pedagogy that the model curriculum describes as "key" and "can be used in ethnic studies research and instruction."[135]

In view of CRT's tenets, Mari Barke, like Emily Ortiz-Wichmann, has called CRT a Marxist doctrine. The CSBA defends CRT by saying that it is not Marxist, but then admits, "CRT was developed by left-leaning legal scholars, some of whom were neo-Marxists."

No wonder, then, that Mari has said, "It is the fact that the same people who are demanding that we implement this Marxist doctrine in our schools also want to prevent us from educating the public about this anti-American prescription of CRT."

CRT, she says, "pits children against each other who would normally love each other." "Children don't see color," she notes, but CRT tells one child "that they're oppressed and the other that they are the oppressor."

"Even the parents who were thought to be oppressed aren't happy either," she says, because "they don't want their child to think they can't excel."

"And these poor people who were told that they're oppressors when they've never done a mean or horrible thing in their life is terrible," she laments, and "when I see people apologizing for their white privilege, it's just so sad that they've been taught that that's what they should be doing."

Barke, however, is optimistic because she says that parents are more motivated and energized than ever to change what is being taught to their children.

"These mama bears," she observed, "you have never seen them as activated as they are now."

She points to the recall of the San Francisco school board members in 2022. "It wasn't like 52 percent" in favor of the recall, "it was 75 percent."

"I think people are awake," she says, and "I'm more hopeful than ever that parents will take back the school boards and we'll have people running those districts who actually care about the kids and care about education."

CHAPTER 11
From Parent to School Board Member to Grassroots Organizer: Tiffany Justice

"Mom" is a powerful word. It connotes a woman whose utmost identity and sacred responsibilities are to her child(ren). In today's sociocultural obsession with gender and race identities, motherhood is sometimes put on the back burner and even replaced with the dehumanizing term "birthing person." This intentional devaluation is a constant reminder of the ironically self-conflicting nature of critical race theory, which has some of its theoretical roots in radical feminism.

What do moms do when confronted with a popular culture that diminishes traditional family values and their role in directing their children's upbringing?

The story of Tiffany Justice, a stay-at-home mom of four who first served at her local school board and then co-founded the "Moms for Liberty" national movement championing parental rights, underscores the vital contributions of *moms* – not political operatives, not activists – in fighting against CRT and its varied mutations.

Born in New York City, Justice moved to Florida at the age of eight with her parents and five siblings, two of whom were adopted. Her parents were actively involved in her and her siblings' education, directing how they were schooled "in the drivers' seat."

After leaving college, she settled down with her own family of six. She devoted herself to raising one girl and three boys, while helping her husband's construction business in sales and marketing. All her kids have gone into the public school system due to the unaffordability of private education.

She first got involved in her oldest daughter's school as a parent volunteer trying to fix the school's dire physical conditions. After a failed attempt to lobby the school principal for much-needed repairs to solve flooding, leaking ceilings, and classrooms in violation of codes, she led a small group of moms and organized school tours for all the school board members and other school district leaders.

When she was told that the school district could just shut down the school and redirect all students from the island on which she lived to the mainland in the same school district, she used her newly acquired knowledge of capital planning, outlay and school funding mechanisms to persuade the school district to renovate the school instead. At the same time, she also helped expose other emerging problems in the school, such as teachers who were ill-equipped to educate underserved students, who lacked foundational skills for reading and couldn't even hold their pencils correctly.

She realized that the school district needed a leadership change and students deserved better than being pushed forward from grade to grade without reaching basic academic proficiencies.

Her successful local organizing effort rallied support and respect from other parents who encouraged her to run for the school board herself, running "as a parent, not a politician":

> If you met me for five minutes, you would
> know no one owns me. You cannot buy me and

I am not willing to play any political game.
School board races are nonpartisan. I want to
invest in public schools for our community.

Once elected, she demanded a rigorous progress monitoring system and higher standards in academic performance, professional development and community outreach.

Indian River County was still under a five-decades-old legal desegregation order, issued in 1967 as a result of a lawsuit against the school district brought by four parents of Black students. This meant the school district was mandated by federal courts to increase the racial integration and educational opportunities of Black and Latino students.

In July 2017, she worked with her colleagues to reach an agreement with the local NAACP, though the NAACP objected to ending the desegregation order on the basis of persisting racial disparities in student achievement and workforce retainment.[136]

When she saw that only 28 percent of the Black students in her district were reading at grade level, she felt "angry for African-American parents in our county." She refused to accept inaction and political bickering for the blatant policy failure, and zeroed in onto the rarely exposed and inconvenient problem of low standards.

There was a multicultural achievement committee where members congregated to discuss cash stipends for teachers and cultural events. She criticized the committee's lack of professionalism and obsession with racial favors, as hinderances for student achievement. Rather than blaming systemic racism or institutional inequity, she said low expectations were a soft bigotry that perpetuated educational disparities and held these students back.

During her term, the school district, like other Florida school districts, saw an influx of state and federal funding earmarked for DEI, SEL, and mental health counseling, in the wake of the 2018 mass shooting tragedy at Marjory Stoneman Douglas High School.

As they are now, these reactionary policy instruments were trojan horses for indoctrination. An automation system called iReady was also introduced to replace traditional instruction and teacher evaluations. Parents were not given access to the software, fueling a frustration that "the learning modules are being used as a babysitter in place of teaching."

Describing the situation as "100 percent programming," she remembered the beginning of the ideological invasion. Context-based learning was replaced by mechanical memorization. She recalled her then fifth-grade son being asked to read and analyze the Four Corners speech without any background knowledge on World War II or the Holocaust.

Also, uninformed school board members become easy prey for national curriculum developers and education nonprofits that offer experimental teaching resources such as SEL for free. When these locally elected members realize that they've allowed indoctrination to take hold in their local communities, it is usually too late.

After serving on the board for a full four-year term, she decided not to run for reelection but did not give up the mission to reform public education.

This time, she would be carrying this mission out at the national stage. In late 2020, she linked up with another lone wolf, Tina Descovich who had served on the Brevard County School Board in Florida during the same time period. Alarmed by the nonstop drum beat of racial divisions and concerned about negative impacts of school closures, they started Moms for Liberty to empower parents, community members and school board members overcome collective action problems.

In January 2021, their fledgling grassroots group started with two chapters in Indian River County and Brevard County. Volunteer moms in the founding chapters would spend countless hours, oftentimes into the early morning, discussing problems facing their local schools and brainstorming on solutions.

By word of mouth, Moms for Liberty ventured out of Florida, with moms from all over the country, worried about the same problems, calling to inquire about starting their own local chapters. As of May 2022, Moms for Liberty had 186 chapters in 35 states with over 85,000 members. Justice welcomed the expansion because "maybe we will be stronger if we invite the whole country to join us." Their mission is to unify, educate and empower parents to defend their parental rights at every level of the government.

Its success, in a large part, can be attributed to a bottom-up approach that pulls back the "education curtain" for everyday American moms and dads. Correctly conceptualizing public education as a largely local affair, Moms for Liberty advocates for parents as "the expert in your own community." When local decision making in school boards and in city or county governments is reclaimed by local experts, meaningful and lasting changes across the country will become a reality.

Moms, regardless of race, intuitively see through the deception of indoctrination, CRT and the interrelated gender ideology, all of which are not result-based and encourage "constantly adversarial engagement."

For instance, during her tenure on the Indian River County Board of Education, she noticed that there were no measurable outcomes for the school district's work in equity and culturally relevant teaching. The only real outcome was to promote ideologically driven teaching practices which are deeply divisive."

Instead of celebrating a common national culture, American children and their parents are racially re-segregated in classroom instruction, community engagement, and interpersonal interactions. Increasingly, unserious proposals for teaching White kids a certain way, Black kids a different way and Asian kids another way are being considered.

"Surely, CRT, the law school course, is not being taught in elementary schools," she says. "But our children are being taught that they should judge each other first by immutable characteristics."

"Moms don't need to be CRT scholars to know that racism and discrimination are bad, no matter who is doing it and for what reason." Every child deserves to be treated equally in school and every child is capable of success in the classroom, if given the right tools. Lowering standards in the name of equity is not the recipe for student success. Parental engagement is.

Student success in retaining foundational knowledge and building skills is severely impeded by CRT, which has now been "forced into every aspect of education." In turn, ideological finger pointing becomes "an excuse for educational failure," falsely attributing the academic achievement gap to racism or inequity.

The ideology of race essentialism is not only unpopular among American adults, it is also resisted by many American children who naturally have diverse friends in a multiracial society. However, she says, the ideologues prey on impressionable youngsters, "cashing in on their inherent empathy for others" and pitting them against each other.

For too long, she says, "parents have been pushed out of" the education decision-making process. Policy wonks, politically driven unions and a ballooning bureaucracy lead to seemingly insurmountable obstacles for parents without fancy graduate degrees to obtain key information and participate in the process related to their children's future.

"What if a mom had an 8th degree education? Why would you ever deny a parent's input in their children's education?," she observes.

Parents should not be treated as a hindrance to the education system or be told that others know better about their children, but they are. In San Diego, recently, a biracial father who appears White in appearance was told to hold off his White male perspective and not question a Black educator's oppression, when asking important questions about the school district's racial equity programming and its ethnic studies courses.[137] This very father's fifth great grandfather fought in the Civil War as an escaped slave.

For Justice, moms should absolutely be in the driver's seat: "I was pregnant for 36 months of my life. I breastfed each one of my children for a year each. I have made thousands of medical decisions for them."

For the generation of moms like Tiffany, who were raised in the 1980s and 1990s, colorblindness, or the spirit of judging someone based on character rather than skin color, is a fundamental American virtue. Aside from race, we have "a million things in common," growing up listening to the same music and watching the same shows. To Tiffany, this is the very best of being an American. But what has been happening in our public life and in our children's schools feels like a betrayal of this belief.

> We got married and we have biracial children. And we thought we lived in a country where skin color didn't matter. We send our kids to schools, where they'd be asked to pick a parent who's oppressed. I think my generation feels lied to – we were promised a colorblind vision but now we are told colorblindness is a trait of white supremacy. Moms are mad and we can see through this nonsense.

That's why Justice and her co-founders of Moms for Liberty dedicate themselves to giving moms the confidence to reclaim parental rights: "Every parent has the fundamental right to direct the upbringing of his or her children. The government does not give you those rights and neither do they have the right to take them away."

In its first year of operations, Moms for Liberty worked with the Florida State Legislature to introduce pro-parent legislation, one of which became the landmark "Parental Rights in Education" bill (HB 1557). The bill, reinforces the fundamental right of parents to "make decisions regarding the upbringing and control of their children," enhances parental access to education and healthcare decisions.[138]

The State of Florida has been leading the charge against the woke culture invasion. The political climate in Florida has been ideal, where Gov. Ron DeSantis has been emboldened by parents and parent advocacy groups represented by Moms for Liberty to pursue parental rights as a key policy issue.

Going into its second year, she emphasized outreach to parents in her organization's activities. Recognizing that many Hispanic families share similar values on family, religion and education, Moms for Liberty recently hired a Director of Hispanic Outreach to get out their pro-parent message in Spanish. Ultimately, this is a unifying message.

In 2021, a Moms for Liberty chapter in West Tennessee launched a grassroots campaign against a DEI-themed K-5 English language curriculum named "Let's Talk Wit and Wisdom." Local moms spent over 1,200 hours into reading the curriculum and uncovered strong evidence of CRT, SEL, suicide ideation and violence.[139]

The group cited four particular books intended for second graders, which replaced teaching of civil rights with explicitly violent and divisive contents, race determinism and stereotyping. While the group's subsequent civil rights complaint to the Tennessee Department of Education contains specific references to problematic writings in these books, theses moms were slandered as reactionary book burners and sympathizers to white supremacy.[140]

Parents have a justifiable right to condemn the practice of allowing problematic and divisive contents in their children's schools. Moms for Liberty, as well as other emerging pro-parent grassroots groups such as No Left Turn in Education and Parents Defending Education, is expanding its base to help sunshine the facts and spread the truth about parental rights.

Having established a strong base of operations in its first year, Moms for Liberty is now working to lobby different state legislatures with legislation supporting parental rights and help local moms organize school board races. They want parents' "fundamental right to direct the upbringing of their children" to be recognized at the state level and at the same time, hold local education leaders accountable for bad decision-making. "That's the way forward in this country," she says.

Justice observes that the majority of American teachers are as frustrated as the public about the counterproductive thought indoctrination going on in public education. Moms for Liberty is also reaching out to teachers to encourage them to come forth with information as whistleblowers and to empower them in this noble profession.

Reflecting on a townhall forum in which she debated a college professor of race studies, she emphasizes the importance of letting teachers focus on teaching the kids and putting the other responsibilities back to the family:

> Schools cannot be everything to everyone. As parents, we recognize there are responsibilities that go along with rights and we ought to own these responsibilities. It is about time America stand up and say: schools cannot raise your children for you. Every American parent needs to think about what the boundary is between school and home. And they need to exert their power to direct their children's upbringing. They must draw a line and then hold it. If every parent starts doing this, the education establishment will have no choice but to recede from encroaching on parental rights.

CHAPTER 12
Taking Back School Boards:
Ryan Girdusky

When it comes to defending what America is really about - a place with endless opportunities and abundant rewards for hard work, it is not just moms and dads joining hands. Grandparents, uncles, aunts, cousins, and other ordinary Americans are also on the front line.

The chief architect of this story is just that. Ryan Girdusky is a college drop-out from Queens, New York. He comes from a working-class family background and has a lot of school-aged cousins, nieces, and nephews in his large Italian-American family.

In 2021, after witnessing children in his big family being compelled to adopt a race-centric, oversimplified view on the American society, he embarked on his own journey to save America's cornerstone values.

He recalls local schools' big push for the anti-police, anti-racism agenda after the killing of George Floyd and his godson's school assignment being the controversial book *Race Cars: A children's book about white privilege*. At the same time, his local community is home to a large population of police officers and first responders.

His family members were outraged by over-the-top school programming and participated at school parent-teacher association meetings and school board meetings to no avail.

Driven by a pure desire to save American public education and our constitutional democratic republic, he started a national political action committee to campaign for anti-CRT school board candidates throughout the country in May 2021. The organization, 1776 Project PAC, is "the only super PAC in the country that pushes against CRT at school board elections." Written on the 1776 Project PAC website:

> We are a political action committee dedicated to electing school board members nationwide who want to reform our public education system by promoting patriotism and pride in American history. We are committed to abolishing critical race theory and 'The 1619 Project' from the public school curriculum.[141]

Distinguishing the organization as an election-focused one rather than a think tank, he confirmed that 1776 Project won 42 of 58 school board races it invested in in 2021.

His work has definitely filled a strategic vacuum. All politics is local, but low voter turnout in local elections reached a crisis proportion over the last several years. According to the "Who Votes for Mayor" project, fewer than 15 percent of eligible voters turn out for mayoral elections in 10 of America's 30 largest cities.[142]

School board elections, outcomes of which largely influence the overall landscape of local education, fared even worse, with a devastating range of 5 to 10 percent in voter turnout between 2014 and 2019.[143]

Since 2020, more and more voters have been showing up at local ballot boxes, energized by education issues such as political indoctrination and school reopening. In addition, more electoral contestation has taken place to effectively challenge incumbents.

For instance, San Dieguito Union High School District held a special election in November 2021 with a notable 19.1 percent voter turnout.[144] From 2018 to 2021, the percentage of unopposed seats in 3,319 school board elections decreased from 40 percent to 24 percent, and seats won by newcomers challenging incumbents increased from 39 percent of the total available seats to 49 percent.[145]

For Girdusky, the mission of the 1776 Project is not to re-make public education, but rather to effectively revive public education through local political contestation. Even though in his own words, he was "a terrible student who suffered from ADHD and not a philosophically deep person," he wants to fight for students so that they can "enjoy and love school."

There is an ingrained notion of citizenship that motivates Girdusky. He sees a well-functioning public education system is part of "public good" that undergirds "a cohesive society" where "we are all invested in part in one another."

> I don't have children, but I still pay for other people's children to go to school. Why? Because I want two things. I want them to love the country. And I want them to be capable enough to join society as a functioning adult and get a job.

The 1776 Project takes on CRT because it is an "overarching issue" that reorients the trajectory of education toward pushing an activist political agenda. CRT in practice infiltrates public schools under the banner of expanding the teaching of history from the perspective of the marginalized.

But it is "the tip of the spear" with an intent to transform the entire system of liberal self-governance by way of indoctrination and also through attacks on merit by destroying of gifted and talented programs in the name of diversity, equity, and inclusion.

He argues that "to advocates of critical race theory, the goal is not the child's betterment. The goal is a political movement to replace the way we operate as a country."

To accomplish the revolutionary objective of transformation, an essentially Marxist goal, proponents have seized the meanings of "very easily understood terms" and "won the language wars." By reframing everyday conversations on complex social and cultural issues into simplistic euphemisms like "diversity," "equity," and "justice," the ideologues emotionally blackmail well-intentioned and unsuspecting people who do not want to be accused of political heresy. That is the very definition of ideological capture.

CRT zealots have established a faulty baseline of understanding, that is "America is an inherently racist society and the fabric of our government is to tear down non-White people especially." Capitalism, parenthood, nuclear family, and even the Constitution are all features of an oppressive system. He makes a hyperbole to illustrate this:

> Everything from the capitalist system that brings you your Apple Computer and your Pepsi Cola to your local representative, to the media you are watching every day is working against you at all times. Oh, and you might not actually be the gender you were born in, and you should hate your parents.

This radical proposal for systemic changes goes against a broader societal consensus for incremental reforms. To Girdusky, "the garden variety Americans" treat education as "an investment into the next generation" and want all kids to succeed. In the event of academic achievement gaps and disparities, most would want to "expand opportunity" and invest public funds wisely so that "children have the most opportunity possible to improve." In other words,

> The majority of Americans want to address
> actual educational issues and make sure
> that children have the most amount of
> opportunities to succeed, rather than worry
> about renaming Thomas Jefferson High
> School or complain that math is racist.

Sadly, this has stifled the common ground of "garden variety Americans." "The more you peel back the onion to see what is going on, the more you realize it is worse than thought." He uses examples from San Francisco, the most liberal city in America, to illustrate the overreach of "the mind-altering ideologues."

In one incident in early 2021, Seth Brenzel, a gay White father of a biracial child, was turned down from his application to serve on a volunteer parent committee at the San Francisco Board of Education. The reason given by the school board was that the father did not enhance the diversity of that volunteer group.[146]

In the other incident, Alison Collins, a former San Francisco Board of Education member and the board's vice president, found issues with the high academic performance of Asian-American students in her district and their "overrepresentation" in the city's elite Lowell High School. To justify her proposal for ending merit-based admission to Lowell[147], Collins accused the Asian-American community of harboring "anti-black racism" and "white-supremacist thinking."

Angered by the board's apparent bigotry and incompetence, and the anti-merit proposal targeting Lowell, San Francisco voters recalled three school board members, including Collins, in a landslide special election held on February 15, 2022. Thirty-six percent of the electorate turned out to vote.[148]

Another trend is the effort to rename schools, school buildings and historic monuments to disassociate from 'racist' or 'oppressive' historical figures. In San Francisco, a project was proposed in early 2021 to rename 44 school, including "Balboa, Lowell and Mission high schools, as well as Roosevelt and Presidio middle schools and Webster, Sanchez and Jose Ortega elementary schools."[149]

Rolled out amidst prolonged school closures and pandemic-induced learning losses, the renaming initiative was rescinded by the school board in April 2021.[150] He observes this phenomenon as an excuse for non-performing schools to continue to fail their students:

> Renaming a school building does not affect the child. It is only a handful of fringe ideologues and academics who think it is more important to find any faint traces of racism, to sniff them out, and to look for them in the cracks and corners than making sure kids learn and excel.

After the San Francisco school board recall, he has strengthened his belief that "we are the majority" and that the other side has gone "too far into the weeds." So, the next question for him is: "who is willing to hear our message?"

Girdusky's strategy includes making the enactment of these policies more expensive and riskier with legal challenges and public pressure campaigns and educating the public about the importance of good cultural values, from hard work to individual liberty.[151]

He and his 1776 Project PAC have utilized the third strategy, the most straightforward one that draws on energetic constituents to produce quick results at the ballot box:

> If you're trying to educate the population on an issue during an election, you're losing them. You're trying to feed on what they already believe and know. Most people in this country believe if you work hard, you should advance regardless of your race. Most people do not support race-based advancement in education. Most people believe in meritocracy, most

people do not believe teachers have the place to talk to young children about sex and sexual orientation. Most people do not believe that this country is an inherently racist and evil place. And most people do not want kids to feel a sense of guilt because of the skin color they were born with. I am just talking to the crowd that already believes that and saying, "Okay, you believe it."

As a unique type of anti-CRT warriors who "deal with it [CRT] on the individual level," Girdusky's 1776 Project makes its decisions for school board elections based on strategic calculations of "cause and effect, action and reaction" rather than grand visions.

He reasons that school board elections are both "nonpartisan and off-cycle." Many are held on "nonpresidential election days in nonpresidential election years" and on odd days to encourage high voter turnout among members of teachers' unions. He uses this intentional design to the advantage of the anti-CRT movement:

I realized that school board elections have an average turnout of about 8% of the electorate. Critical race theory has become an energizing issue on the right, and they care about it. If I were to engage with a certain percentage of the Republican voters who vote in presidential elections or in congressional elections, but maybe not in those off-cycle elections, I could change the turnout in areas that even voted Democrat previously. Especially for nonpartisan races, there's no D or R behind someone's name. So, I focused on turning out five to 10% more Republicans in all these areas.

Focused on how to make more people who are politically active in general elections go vote in school board elections, he knows he is not in the business of "winning hearts and minds" or "changing the world." This sort of grounded pragmatism has proven to be highly effective in accomplishing his two overarching goals: 1. Persuade White children that they are not inherently evil for the skin color they were born into; 2. Make sure all children who work hard can succeed in schools.

Since his new PAC is an emerging organization with a relatively small staff and a small budget, He foregoes candidate training and looks for those who are already motivated to change local education policy making. His strategy is to "give them a little extra push."

When fielding the candidates for the PAC to support through mailers and other campaign methods, He asks hard questions: "How many doors have you knocked? Do you know any voters you need? How many calls have you made? Do you have a mailer coming out? Do you have texting coming out?"

Surprisingly, the biggest supporters behind his new operation have been "big Democrats" who donated to Joe Biden and other Democratic candidates. He attributes this to the nonpartisan nature of most Americans and their growing distaste for these policies:

> They genuinely want good schools. They want small businesses to thrive. They want some kind of health care apparatus in case people get very, very sick. They don't want people to fall into deep poverty. They want clean streets, no potholes and want criminals to go to prison when they commit a crime. They want good schools.

The silent majority is mobilizing behind a great cause to save America from ideological suicide. He noted that most of his liberal donors support the 1776 Project because they are fed up with what is going on in schools but cannot go on the offense publicly.

While his strategic considerations have been on target, his track record of 42 electoral victories out of 58 school board races in the first year also derived from his past working experience as a writer and political consultant.

A college drop-out, he started working in politics professionally at the young age of 19. For a few years, he was immersed in New York politics, working for the city council and then for the state senate. In 2009, he campaigned for Michael Bloomberg's successful mayoral race. Later, he was an opinion writer for the *Washington Examiner* and author.

In 2021, he noticed the rapid spread of anti-racism indoctrination in public schools and the relative silence of conservatives who at the time had limited their attention to school choice:

> Prominent critical race theorists often cloak their ideology with the phrase "anti-racism," a popular strategy of far-left-wing activist Ibram X. Kendi. "The heartbeat of racism is denial. And too often, the more powerful the racism, the more powerful the denial," Kendi says. In other words, Kendi (and those who agree with him) frame the issue as either being pro-critical race theory (or anti-racist) or pro-racism. Children instructed under critical race theory are taught one key thing: All ideas central to America's founding are a farce.[152]

Years of ploughing and working in the field has earned Girdusky valuable connections and insights that have helped the 1776 Project take off quickly. But it has brought fierce pushback from hostile media platforms.

The *Daily Beast* accused him of being part of a "far-right snitch network target[ing] schools that talk about race"[153] and another opinion piece smeared him as anti-Black.

Local media from the places where the 1776 Project funded its endorsed candidates also wrote negative pieces on him.

Some candidates he had backed could not withstand the media firestorm – they either quit or dissociated themselves from him. In Kansas City, Missouri, a 1776-backed candidate dropped out of the race, two months before the election, due to the pressure of harassment and bullying. In New Jersey, some of the candidates supported by the PAC started attacking his anti-CRT positions.

He has his eyes set on the big picture, to turn out "a sliver of the electorate" who only need to be nudged a little bit. And these people will not be deterred by media hyperboles:

> Most people don't care really what the media says. The media builds an overarching narrative, but the people are not going to care who Ryan Girdusky from Queens, New York is. The media is not going to decide how people vote in Colorado, Minnesota or Kansas.

Despite challenges and media caricatures, the 1776 Project had a huge success in 2021, helping 72 percent of endorsed candidates win school board positions, even in deep blue counties and flipping 18 school boards from union-backed majorities.

In Shenandoah County Public Schools in Woodstock, Virginia, a 19-year-old college freshman named Kyle Gutshall won the District 4 school board seat, along with two other candidates, on a pro-parent, anti-CRT slate backed by PACs, including the 1776 Project.[154] He attributed Kyle's landslide election result of winning 59.5 percent of the votes to hard work and good values.

Like Shenandoah County, Johnson County in Kansas and Douglas County in Colorado are traditionally progressive counties where he invested the resources of his PAC for slates of school board candidates:

> If we can win more suburban districts, that would be great. We want to gradually take

over the elite public schools in Long Island or in Northern Virginia or in parts of California, in those elite areas where public schools affect private schools. That's really where our efforts have to be doubled up.

In Kansas, seven of 10 local candidates backed by the 1776 Project won their races in November 2021.[155] Among them, two candidates for the Blue Valley school board in Johnson County ran as a conservative slate. One of them, Kaety Bowers, pledged to remove the teaching of CRT, in the form of diversity, equity, and inclusion training and improve academic performance.

In Douglas County, Colorado, four newly elected anti-CRT board members managed to secure a 4-to-3 vote in February, 2022 to remove the district superintendent who had supported the incorporation of equity and CRT in local schools.[156] This is a strong case in point for his school board strategy.

Deep down, Girdusky has a patriotic and almost poetic view about what his efforts means for America, in spite of seeing himself as "not philosophical."

> No country in the world has not had their growing pains. No region of the world was exempt from the historical stains of slavery or indentured servitude. The bad things about human society and human nature are not intrinsically tied to being an American, being Western, being White, or being European.
>
> In America, we have been and should be continually teaching children history, slavery, the Trail of Tears, Jim Crow, the Chinese Exclusion Act... But the overarching baseline should be the greatness of America, that it is a great country that has advanced justice, liberty and equality. We are the great equalizer.

When it comes to defending America's founding values, he warns against the cultural and social destructions of these policies:

> This society that we built is not by accident. You weren't born into something that just happened to be prosperous, safe and wonderful. It took a long time and a lot of suffering to get here. But societies created over long periods of time can be destroyed very quickly. We need to appreciate it, learn from it, understand the greatness of this society and the men and women who died and invested every fiber of their being, their fortune, their energy, their life to create this wonderful place.

Like other critics of CRT, he also disapproves the dogma's pessimistic and over-simplifying diagnosis that structural inequities and racism are to blame for current disparities. After all, the economic growth and social mobility of Black Americans were unprecedented following the end of the Civil War. The story of immense "prosperity and creation of culture" has been overlooked in CRT's overhanging narrative of victimhood.

> If we were to really change the way we talk about history, along with conversations about slavery and Jim Crow, we need to talk more about the explosion in opportunity and the explosion in great talent and entrepreneurship that came out of the black community post-Civil War. Unfortunately, the idea of overarching acceptance and growth is one story being lost.

Also, he sees the Asian-American community in Queens, New York as another example of the successful American experiment. Their story of rising up from "one of the poorest circumstances" to overwhelming success within a generation through hard work and education should not be brushed off as just a model minority hype.

But thanks to his relentless efforts at the local level, the chance for us to reclaim the idea of color blindness, to fight for every American child to be treated equally without regard to race, is now higher than just a couple of years ago.

He also has some practical suggestions for those who want to make a difference in their local communities. First, parents and concerned citizens should get all the relevant information: "if your kid comes home with an insane homework, take a photograph of it and get copies of everything to distribute to other parents."

Public engagement should be done civilly, no matter how outrageous the circumstances. Last but not least, people can reach out to Girdusky if they are willing to put in the hard work to run and take over their local school boards, one of the basic institutions of our democratic system.

CONCLUSION
Overcoming Division and Unifying America

While progressives claim that critical race theory is just a legal theory and is not used as the basis for K-12 classroom instruction, the personal stories contained in this book tell us emphatically that race-based indoctrination in the classroom is not just some theory, but an all-too-frequent reality.

Indeed, as progressives in the media, academia, and public-school systems bob, weave, and obfuscate, real people are being hurt, starting with our nation's children.

Joshua's experience as a middle school student has become far too common. Despite his biracial and multicultural heritage, his individuality was ignored as he was singled out as privileged based on his perceived race. He was also denounced loudly, like in the Cultural Revolution in Communist China, by his classmates for using the "wrong" pronoun in reference to another student.

Equity, which means producing the same student outcomes regardless of race, is now the guiding mantra at schools, even though, as Joshua points out, "having the perfectly same outcome for every group is pretty much wholly unrealistic."

Yet, in the name of equity, schools like Joshua's have dumbed down their education programs—eliminating honors and advanced classes, dropping citizenship grades, allowing multiple re-takes of exams, and reducing grading requirements. Instead, schools are pushing exercises aimed at battling supposed white supremacy traits, such as factual objectivity.

No one at his school acknowledges that these changes are based on critical race theory, says Joshua. Rather, they are explained as privilege activities, social emotional learning activities, or equity activities.

Joshua said that he used to like school when it valued knowledge and excellence, but he is now resentful because every day "becomes more and more of a challenge and more exhausting because we go to school and it's like a battleground."

"I'm not coming to school to learn about social justice or activism," he implores. Yet, regardless of his preferences, the ideological agenda of adults in public school systems is being imposed on students like him and countless others across the country.

In response to this ideological revolution in the classroom, parents have fought back. The heroic parents profiled in this book have shown the many ways that moms and dads from coast to coast are fighting for the future of their children.

These parents have used an array of tactics to counter the race-based politicization of their children's schools. For example, some have gone to court.

Gabs Clark, a low-income African-American mom living in a Las Vegas motel, filed a lawsuit in federal court when her son's high school withheld his diploma after he refused to complete racial privilege exercises.

Asra Nomani, the Muslim mom born in India whose father marched with Mahatma Gandhi, was part of the lawsuit challenging the alleged anti-Asian admissions system at her son's high school in Virginia.

Other parents focused on exposing what was really taking place in their children's classrooms.

Rhode Island mom Nicole Solas used public record requests to expose the race-based teachings in her daughter's school after the school staff hid the curriculum from her. For her efforts to bring transparency for parents, she was sued by the local teachers' union. But she has not backed down.

On the other side of the country, California mom Kelly Schenkoske used public record requests to find school district documents that constantly cited and referenced critical race theory.

Other parents have run for their local school board.

Florida mom Tiffany Justice ran for her school board, won, and fought the incompetency of her district's school establishment.

Southern California moms Mari Barke and Emily Ortiz-Wichmann were elected to their school boards and have used their positions to fight critical race theory and other race-based pedagogies.

Ryan Girdusky started a political action committee that is solely devoted to electing pro-reform school board members. He has had incredible success in states across the country, including recent historic victories across Florida.

Girdusky says[157] that parents "don't want schools to sit there and indoctrinate children" and they "don't want schools to sit there and apply critical race theory or critical gender theory to their children."

Moms and dads have also started local, state, and national grassroots parent organizations.

Elana Fishbein, an Israeli immigrant born to Sephardic Jewish parents, founded No Left Turn in Education, which was the first organization to organize parents to speak out at their local school board meetings against race-based curriculum.

Elina Kaplan, an immigrant from the former Soviet Union, and Lia Rensin, whose grandfather survived the Holocaust, are leaders in the Alliance for Constructive Ethnic Studies, which opposes efforts to use ethnic studies in schools as a means to introduce race-based radicalism into the classroom.

Tiffany Justice started Moms for Liberty, which has grown into a powerful national organization.

The bottom line is that moms and dads are spearheading an education revolution that emphasizes balanced non-ideological instruction, transparency, and parental control. While the education establishment snuck critical race theory and its various permutations into classrooms, parents are getting informed, are fighting back, and are now starting to win.

Perhaps the people who are the most determined to fight Marxist-inspired race indoctrination in the classroom are those whose family or themselves have escaped from communism.

The authors of this book interviewed Joe Nalven, a cultural anthropologist who served as associate director of the Institute for Regional Studies of the Californias at San Diego State University. Joe's grandparents came to America from Eastern Europe. The influence of communism was strong in his family and Joe was named after Joseph Stalin, the notorious Soviet dictator who was responsible for the deaths of millions.

Because of his varied experiences as an observer, investigator, and researcher. Joe deeply appreciates the natural diversity and intricacy of human interactions. It is also why he opposes critical race theory.

The simplistic dichotomy of oppressor versus victim is what connects CRT with Marxism, neo-Marxism, and communism. "The camaraderie of the oppressed," he says, fuels the ideological battles against "capitalism, Eurocentric thinking, and colonialism."

He observes that the oppression mindset undercuts nuanced thinking and interpretation of consequential issues: "Instead of having this universality of identity, and individuality, you have basically a grievance, victim-oriented oppression kind of framework that only focuses on four different races."

With his background as a cultural anthropologist, Joe testified against a CRT-influenced curriculum pushed by a San Diego-area school district. While his criticisms were directed at a particular curriculum, they can be applied generally to most such curricula. He pointed out that the curriculum ignored "social change that overcomes that oppression; it minimizes individual achievement for the collective grievance of the four foundational and other racialized groups; it ignores the motivation of immigrants who are drawn to this country for its opportunity, freedom, better living conditions, and family reunification."

Two of Joe's recommendations to address the battles over curricula can be implemented in any school district in the country: 1) Insist on viewpoint diversity, which is the essence of liberal democracy, and 2) Create an ongoing community panel that gives voice to important differences and that promotes transparency.

Voters should know what school board members stand for, as it might ultimately mean that the best recourse is to launch a lawsuit. Those are two of the key remedies that the parents profiled in this book have used with initial and promising effectiveness.

Perhaps the most chilling warnings about critical race theory and race-based indoctrination came from Xi Van Fleet, the Virginia mom who emigrated from Communist China after living through the hell on earth of Mao Zedong's infamous Cultural Revolution, which killed millions of ordinary Chinese people.

During the Cultural Revolution, radicalized young people became Red Guards who beat, humiliated, and killed those perceived to be enemies of Mao and Communist ideology.

The Black Book of Communism, which is the most authoritative history of communism in the 20th Century, describes a brainwashed ten-year-old boy who denounced his father saying:

> You are a counterrevolutionary and a disgrace
> to the family. You have caused grave losses to
> the government. It serves you right that you
> are in prison. All I can say is that you better

reform yourself well, or you will get what you deserve.[158]

Van Fleet grew up in China during this evil and dark period. She saw posters at her school and remembered: "I could see the illustrations of denunciations and struggles." At first, it seemed like just propaganda, but "it got violent as school kids, aged between six and twelve, started to attack teachers."

She witnessed the Red Guards, who were mostly middle and high school-aged students, raid homes of supposed anti-revolutionaries to destroy anything that connoted old ideas, old culture, old customs, and old habits.

She herself was sent away from her family in the city to work as a farm laborer for three years. She said, "Nobody wanted to be sent to the countryside to endure exile and hardship, but I tried to tell myself that I was not very woke and I did not have class consciousness."

Van Fleet immigrated to America to find freedom. Yet, today she sees her adopted country starting to mimic the ideological totalitarianism of Maoist China. She has been accused of being privileged for living in a middle-class neighborhood. Yet, she emphasizes, "How can you tell me, someone who suffered so much and was actually oppressed under Mao's Communist rule, that I don't understand what oppression is?"

What she sees happening in America is eerily similar to what happened in China. People are being divided into classes. While people in China were divided into classes based on economic status, people in America are being divided into classes based on race. Because American capitalism has created prosperity and upward mobility, she says, "the best way to divide America is by race."

She says that students are being indoctrinated to become warriors in the name of social justice, diversity, equity, inclusion, and anti-racism. They are becoming, she believes, almost like current-day Red Guards. She laments, "this is something that I never thought I would see in America."

The result, according to Van Fleet, is the suppression of free speech, which was a hallmark of the Cultural Revolution. In Communist China, she recalled, "Anything you say can be taken as anti- or counter-revolutionary." Today in America, "anything you say that somehow does not line up with this narrative, you are a racist."

"In China, we were taught at a very young age to just shut up," she said. Across America, large majorities of students acknowledge self-censoring.

She concludes, "Everything that's going on here happened in China during the Cultural Revolution." Given that critical race theory has its roots in Marxism, she declares, "It should have no place in our schools."

To the American people, she says, if you do not speak up "the next thing you will lose is your freedom and the next thing may be your life." Thus, "you can't pretend nothing is happening and wish it would just go away" because "it won't go away."

"We have to get involved," she urges.

The people profiled in this book have gotten involved. They are true American heroes who are rallying Americans to not only save our youth, but to save the country itself.

The Pledge of Allegiance says that our nation is indivisible. Americans must therefore unite as one people again to reclaim our schools and our culture before it is too late.

ENDNOTES

1   Carol Swain and Christopher Schorr, *Black Eye for America* (Rockville, MD: Be the People Books, 2021), p. 12.

2   Ibid, pp. 12-13.

3   Ibid, p. 13.

4   Ibid.

5   Julie Barrett, "How To See If Critical Race Theory Is In Your Kids' School—And Fight It," *The Federalist*, August 18, 2021, available at https://thefederalist.com/2021/08/18/how-to-see-if-critical-race-theory-is-in-your-kids-school-and-fight-it/

6   Ibid.

7   Ibid.

8   Ibid.

9   Allan Bloom, *The Closing of the American Mind*, New York: Simon & Schuster Inc. (1987), 19.

10 Ibid, 29.

11 Wenyuan Wu, "Should I Get Canceled for Telling the Emperor He Has No Clothes On?" *Minding the Campus*, March 1, 2021, https://www.mindingthecampus.org/2021/03/01/should-i-get-canceled-for-telling-the-emperor-he-has-no-clothes-on/.

12 Christopher F. Rufo, "Bad Education," *City Journal*, February 11, 2021, https://www.city-journal.org/philadelphia-fifth-graders-forced-to-celebrate-black-communism.

13 Californians for Equal Rights Foundation, "Empirical Data on Diversity, Equity and Inclusion and Critical Race Theory," accessed March 28, 2022, https://cferfoundation.org/crt-in-school-districts/.

14 Michael Ruiz, "California group files federal civil rights complaint over San Diego school district's 'racist' teachings," *Fox News*, April 17, 2021, https://www.foxnews.com/us/california-federal-civil-rights-complaint-san-diego-school-district.

15 Ibram X. Kendi, "There Is No Debate Over Critical Race Theory," *The Atlantic*, July 9, 2021, https://www.theatlantic.com/ideas/archive/2021/07/opponents-critical-race-theory-are-arguing-themselves/619391/.

16   Reject Critical Race Theory, "Debunking CRT," accessed March 28, 2022, https://www.rejectcrt.org/debunking-crt.

17   Janel George, "A Lesson on Critical Race Theory," *The American Bar Association*, January 11, 2021, https://www.americanbar.org/groups/crsj/publications/human_rights_magazine_home/civil-rights-reimagining-policing/a-lesson-on-critical-race-theory/.

18   Kendi, "There Is No."

19   Roy L. Brooks, "Critical Race Theory: A Proposed Structure and Application to Federal Pleading," *Harvard BlackLetter Law Journal*, Spring, 1994, 11.

20   Richard Delgado & Jean Stefancic, *Critical race theory: an introduction (Third ed.)* 2017, 1.

21   Ibid.

22   Katy Steinmetz, "She Coined the Term 'Intersectionality' Over 30 Years Ago. Here's What It Means to Her Today," *Time Magazine*, February 20, 2020, https://time.com/5786710/kimberle-crenshaw-intersectionality/.

23   Peter McLaren, "Critical pedagogy: A look at the major concepts," In Antonia Darder et al. (Eds.), *The critical pedagogy reader* (pp. 69-96). New York and London: Routlege/Falmer.

24   Gloria Ladson-Billings and William F. Tate IV, "Toward a Critical Race Theory of Education," *Teachers College Record* Vol. 97, no. 1, Fall 1995, 62.

25   Helen Pluckrose and James Lindsay, *Cynical Theories: How Activist Scholarship Made Everything about Race, Gender, and Identity—and Why This Harms Everybody*, Pitchstone Publishing: Durham, 2020, 128.

26   Erec Smith. *A Critique of Anti-racism in Rhetoric and Composition: The Semblance of Empowerment*, Lexington Books: Lanham, XIV.

27   Ibram X. Kendi, *How to Be an Anti-racist*, One World: New York, 2019, 19

28   "The 1619 Project," *The New York Times Magazine*, August 14, 2019, https://www.nytimes.com/interactive/2019/08/14/magazine/1619-america-slavery.html.

29   "Critical Race Theory: On the New Ideology of Race," *the Manhattan Institute*, December 16, 2020, https://www.manhattan-institute.org/critical-race-theory-new-ideology-race.

30   Carol Swain, "Critical race theory's toxic, destructive impact on America," *1776 Unites*, January 15, 2021, https://1776unites.com/essays/critical-race-theorys-toxic-destructive-impact-on-america/.

31 David North and Eric London, "The 1619 Project and the falsification of history: An analysis of the New York Times' reply to five historians," *World Socialist Web Site*, December 28, 2019, https://www.wsws.org/en/articles/2019/12/28/nytr-d28.html.

32 Glenn Loury, "Whose Fourth of July? Blacks and the 'American project'," *1776 Unites*, February 9, 2021, https://1776unites.com/essays/whose-fourth-of-july-blacks-and-the-american-project/.

33 University of Michigan, "Defining DEI," accessed March 29, 2022, https://diversity.umich.edu/about/defining-dei/.

34 D20 DEI. "What is DEI?" https://d20dei.org/dei/.

35 Larry Ortiz and Jayshree Jani, "Critical Race Theory: A Transformational Model for Teaching Diversity," *Journal of Social Work Education*, 2019, Vol. 46, No. 2, 175.

36 Solano Beach Unified School District. (2021). "Board Policy 0415: Diversity, Equity, and Inclusion."

37 "Proposed Regulatory Action Amending Title 5, of the California Code of Regulations, to Include Diversity, Equity, Inclusion, and Accessibility Standards in the Evaluation and Tenure Review of District Employees," *California Community Colleges*, 2022.

38 Wenyuan Wu, "When Diversity Invades Precision Agriculture," *Minding the Campus*, December 6, 2021, https://www.mindingthecampus.org/2021/12/06/when-diversity-invades-precision-agriculture/.

39 Jay Greene, "Diversity University: DEI Bloat in the Academy," *Heritage Foundation*, July 27, 2021, https://www.heritage.org/education/report/diversity-university-dei-bloat-the-academy.

40 Christian Schneider, "UC Berkeley spends $25M a year, pays 400 employees to advance 'equity and inclusion'," *The College Fix*, April 8, 2021, https://www.thecentersquare.com/california/uc-berkeley-spends-25m-a-year-pays-400-employees-to-advance-equity-and-inclusion/article_65d5a4ec-9894-11eb-b349-4324d0736e41.html.

41 Californians for Equal Rights Foundation, "Empirical Data on."

42 Kim Tran, "The Diversity and Inclusion Industry Has Lost Its Way," *Harper Bazaar*, March 23, 2021, https://www.harpersbazaar.com/culture/features/a35915670/the-diversity-and-inclusion-industry-has-lost-its-way/.

43 Sean Copper, "Getting Rich in the Diversity Marketplace," *Tablet*, April 20, 2021, https://www.tabletmag.com/sections/news/articles/ethnic-studies-diversity-consultants-schools-sean-cooper.

44 Assembly Bill No. 2016, https://leginfo.legislature.ca.gov/faces/billNavClient.xhtml?bill_id=201520160AB2016.

45 "Ethnic Studies Model Curriculum," California Department of Education, updated April 08, 2021, accessed October 26, 2021, https://www.cde.ca.gov/ci/cr/cf/esmc.asp.

46 Lily Button, "Gov. Gavin Newsom signs AB 101, requiring ethnic studies course in public high schools," *The Daily Californian*, October 12, 2021, https://www.dailycal.org/2021/10/12/newsom-signs-ab-101-requiring-ethnic-studies-in-public-high-schools/.

47 Californians for Equal Rights Foundation, "CFER and Three San Diego Parents Sue the State of California for the Aztec and Ashe Prayers in Its Ethnic Studies Model Curriculum," September 3, 2021, https://cferfoundation.org/pr_0903/.

48 LESMC, "Welcome to Liberated Ethnic Studies," http://www.liberatedethnicstudies.org.

49 LESMC, "Critical Race Theory: A Pair of Eyeglasses," http://www.liberatedethnicstudies.org/crt.html.

50 "Memorandum of Understanding Between Our Transformation of Education, R. Tolteka Cuauhtin and Salinas Union High School District for facilitating professional development for Ethnic Studies," https://go.boarddocs.com/ca/salinas/Board.nsf/files/C43NQB60D781/$file/Our%20Transformation%20of%20Education%20MOU%20.pdf.

51 Gabe Stutman, "Castro Valley school board approves contract with 'liberated' ethnic studies group," *Jewish Weekly*, January 20, 2022, https://jweekly.com/2022/01/20/castro-valley-school-board-approves-contract-with-liberated-ethnic-studies-group/

52 Gabe Stutman, "'Liberated' ethnic studies group hit with lawsuit alleging civil rights violations," *Jewish Weekly*, May 13, 2022, https://jweekly.com/2022/05/13/liberated-ethnic-studies-group-hit-with-federal-suit-alleging-civil-rights-violations.

53 Judith Briggs. "Engaging Critical Race Theory and Culturally Relevant Teaching: Preparing White Teacher Candidates to Teach in Urban Environments." *Gauisus*. https://gauisus.weebly.com/briggs---engaging-critical-race-theory-and-culturally-relevant-teaching.html.

54 Cleveland Hayes and Brenda Juarez. (2012). "There is No Culturally Responsive Teaching Spoken Here: A Critical Race Perspective." *Democracy & Education*. Vo; 20, No.1, 1.

55 Collaborative for Academic, Social, and Emotional Learning (CASEL). (2020). "What is SEL?" https://casel.org/what-is-sel/.

56 Haymarket Books. (2020). "Abolitionist Teaching and the future of Our Schools." https://youtu.be/uJZ3RPJ2rNc.

57   Kathy Evans, Brenda Morrison, and Dorothy Vaandering, "Critical Race Theory and Restorative Justice Education," https://zehr-institute.org/publications/docs/chapter-6.pdf.

58   Ibid, 21.

59   Anita K. Wadhwa, "'There Has Never Been a Glory Day in Education for Non-Whites': Critical Race Theory and Discipline Reform in Denver," *International Journal on School Disaffection*, v7 n2 p21-28 2010.

60   Ben & Jerry's Website. "7 Ways We Know Systemic Racism Is Real." https://www.benjerry.com/whats-new/2016/systemic-racism-is-real.

61   CARF. (1998). "What is institutional racism?" *Institute of Race Relations*. https://irr.org.uk/article/what-is-institutional-racism/.

62   National Museum of African American History & Culture. "Being Anti-racist." https://nmaahc.si.edu/learn/talking-about-race/topics/being-antiracist.

63   Ibid.

64   Laura Meckler, "National school board group says it wrongly took sides in political debate," *The Washington Post,* May 21, 2022, https://www.washingtonpost.com/education/2022/05/21/nsba-report-domestic-terrorism-parents/.

65   Helen Raleigh, "The Plaintiff in Brown v. Board Died Before Her Dreams of Education Equality Came True," *The Federalist,* March 28, 2018, available at https://thefederalist.com/2018/03/28/plaintiff-brown-v-board-education-died-dreams-education-equality-came-true/

66   Joshua Dunn, "Critical Race Theory Collides with the Law," *Education Next*, Fall 2021, available at https://www.educationnext.org/critical-race-theory-collides-with-law/

67   Ibid.

68   https://www.educationnext.org/critical-race-theory-collides-with-law/

69   Dunn, op. cit.

70   Ibid.

71   *West Virginia State Board of Education v. Barnette,* 319 U.S. 624 (1943)

72   Dunn, op. cit.

73   See https://www.cfchildren.org/what-is-social-emotional-learning/

74   See https://www.wokekindergarten.org

75   Ibid.

76   Ibid.

77 Darragh Rohe, "Video of White Students Being Told to Leave Multicultural Space Goes Viral," *Newsweek*, September 24, 2021, https://www.newsweek.com/video-white-students-leave-multicultural-space-viral-1632411.

78 Brielle Entzminger, "Unwelcome: Student activists don't want UVA police in their spaces." *C-Ville*, September 29, 2021, https://www.c-ville.com/unwelcome.

79 Megan Burke, "Sisters Calling Attention To Racism In Poway Unified Prompts Changes," *KPBS*, October 26, 2020, https://www.kpbs.org/news/midday-edition/2020/10/26/sisters-instagram-account-calling-attention-racism.

80 Samuel Abrams, "High School Students Value Free Speech but Feel Uncomfortable Speaking Up," *Real Clear Education*, June 3, 2022, https://www.realcleareducation.com/articles/2022/06/03/high_school_students_value_free_speech_but_feel_uncomfortable_speaking_up_110735.html.

81 Maria Carrasco, "Survey: Most Students Self-Censor on Campus and Online," *Insider Higher Ed*, September 23, 2021, https://www.insidehighered.com/quicktakes/2021/09/23/survey-most-students-self-censor-campus-and-online.

82 Jacob Poushter, "40% of Millennials OK with limiting speech offensive to minorities," *Pew Research Center*, November 20, 2015, https://www.pewresearch.org/fact-tank/2015/11/20/40-of-millennials-ok-with-limiting-speech-offensive-to-minorities/.

83 Lizzie May, "Mother sues school after they disciplined her daughter, 7, and forced her to make a public apology for writing 'any life' on a Black Lives Matter drawing," *Daily Mail*, July 13, 2022, https://www.dailymail.co.uk/news/article-11010261/Mother-sues-school-disciplined-daughter-writing-life-BLM-drawing.html.

84 Emily A. Vogels, "A growing share of Americans are familiar with 'cancel culture'," *Pew Research Center*, June 9, 2022, https://www.pewresearch.org/fact-tank/2022/06/09/a-growing-share-of-americans-are-familiar-with-cancel-culture/.

85 Jessica Chasmar and Kelly Laco, "DC school gave 4-year-olds 'anti-racism' 'fistbook' asking them to identify racist family," *Fox News*, May 2, 2022, https://nypost.com/2022/05/02/dc-school-gave-4-year-olds-anti-racism-fistbook-asking-them-to-identify-racist-family/.

86 Richard Bernstein, *Dictatorship of Virtue: How the Battle Over Multiculturalism is Reshaping Our Schools, Our Country, and Our Lives*, Vintage Books, 1995.

87   No Left Turn in Education, "North Carolina Pushed Racialized Preschool Teacher Training While Hiding Evidence." No Left Turn in Education press release, June 8, 2022, https://www.noleft-turn.us/north-carolina-pushed-racialized-training/.

88   Newsmax, "How this dad literally uncovered shocking woke school's parent policy | National Report," YouTube video, 5:34, June 1, 2022, https://www.youtube.com/watch?v=z6fMptat-Wac&t=6s.

89   Asra Nomani, "Asian American students have a target on their backs thanks to critical race theory," *USA Today*, March 26, 2021, available at https://www.usatoday.com/story/opin-ion/2021/03/26/tj-high-school-admissions-race-asian-parents-column/6982183002/

90   "Fighting Race-Based Discrimination at Nation's Top-Ranked High School," Pacific Legal Foundation, available at https://pacifi-clegal.org/case/coalition_for_tj/

91   Asra Nomani and Daniel Kennelly, "A War on Excellence," *City Journal*, September 27, 2021, available at https://www.city-journal.org/asra-q-nomani-on-the-war-on-merit

92   Case 1:21-cv-00296-CMH-JFA, Document 143, February 25, 2022, available at https://pacificlegal.org/wp-content/up-loads/2021/03/Coalition-for-TJ-v.-Fairfax-County-School-Board-Decision.pdf

93   Ibid.

94   Ibid.

95   Ibid.

96   Ibid.

97   Ibid.

98   Ibid.

99   The AMCHA Initiative, "74 Jewish and Education Groups Join Thousands of Petitioners in Demanding Newsom Veto Ethnic Studies Requirement Bill," September 30, 2021, https://amchaini-tiative.org/74-groups-vetoab101-9-30-21pr/.

100   Aaron Bandler, "CA Gov. Says Proposed Ethnic Studies Curric-ulum 'Will Never See the Light of Day'," *Jewish Journal*, August 23, 2019, https://jewishjournal.com/news/california/303507/ca-gov-says-proposed-ethnic-studies-curriculum-will-never-see-the-light-of-day/.

101   Save Arab American Studies, "Remove Names from Ethnic Studies Model Curriculum," February 3, 2021, https://saveara-bamericanstudies.org/wp-content/uploads/2021/02/Letter-to-CDE-2.3.2021.pdf.

102 CFER Foundation, "Act Now! Voice Your Opposition to the Divisive Ethnic Studies Model Curriculum," December 27, 2020, https://cferfoundation.org/act-now-voice-your-opposition-to-the-divisive-ethnic-studies-model-curriculum/.

103 Gabe Stutman, "Everything you need to know about the 'guardrails' built into the California ethnic studies law," The Jewish News of Northern California, October 18, 2021, https://www.jweekly.com/2021/10/18/everything-you-need-to-know-about-the-guardrails-built-into-the-california-ethnic-studies-law/.

104 Ibid.

105 Rasmussen, Scott. "84% Believe Parents Should be Able to See All Curriculum Plans and Materials." *Scott Rasmussen*. February, 22, 2022, https://scottrasmussen.com/ed-transparency/.

106 Ibram X. Kendi, *How to Be an Anti-racist*, One World: New York, 2019, 33-34

107 South Kingstown School Committee. "Jun 02, 2021 – South Kingstown School Committee Special Meeting Agenda." *Board Docs*. https://go.boarddocs.com/ri/soki/Board.nsf/goto?open&id=C3FCZG3379A9

108 Nicole Solas, remarks to South Kingstown School District School Committee, June 2, 2021, https://www.youtube.com/watch?v=4B-GxUD2Rs5g

109 Laura Meckler, "New Transparency Bills Will Force Teachers to Post Instructional Materials," *The Washington Post*, March 2, 2022, https://www.washingtonpost.com/education/2022/03/02/transparency-curriculum-teachers-parents-rights/.

110 KION News Channel, "Parents get heated over SUHSD ethnic studies curriculum at board meeting Tuesday," https://www.youtube.com/watch?app=desktop&v=kf3etLC7RuI#dialog.

111 LATCRIT, "From Critical Legal Legal Theory to Academic Activism," https://latcrit.org/publications/latcrit-primers/.

112 Max Eden, "Critical Race Theory in American Classrooms, *City Journal*, September 18, 2020, available at https://www.city-journal.org/critical-race-theory-in-american-classrooms

113 Stephen Sawchuck, "Local School Boards are Banning Critical Race Theory. Here's How That Looks in 7 Districts," *Education Week*, August 25, 2021, available at https://www.edweek.org/leadership/local-school-boards-are-also-banning-lessons-on-race-heres-how-that-looks-in-7-districts/2021/08

114 William Galston, "A Deeper Look at Critical Race Theory," *Wall Street Journal*, July 20, 2021, available at https://www.wsj.com/articles/kimberle-crenshaw-critical-race-theory-woke-marxism-education-11626793272

115 *Ibid.*

116 *Ibid.*

117 *Ibid.*

118 *Ibid.*

119 Jeff Cook, "Why I'm A Racist," *Huffington Post*, July 16, 2016, available at https://www.huffpost.com/entry/why-im-a-racist_b_57893b9ee4b0e7c873500382

120 Orange County Department of Education, "Special Community Forums on 'California's Ethnic Study Model Curriculum,'" January 5, 2022, available at https://ocbe.us/Documents/Board%20Updates/Policy%20Paper%20on%20Ethnic%20Studies%20and%20Critical%20Race%20Theory%20in%20California.pdf

121 California School Board Association, "Critical Race Theory FAQ," available at https://www.csba.org/-/media/CSBA/Files/GovernanceResources/EducationalEquity/CriticalRaceTheory_FAQ_7-1-2021.ashx

122 Maimon Schwarzschild, "Orange County Board of Education Presentation," available at http://www.newamericancivilrightsproject.org/wp-content/uploads/2021/07/Orange-County-Board-of-Education-Presentation-july-2021academic-circulation.pdf

123 Ibid.

124 Ibid.

125 *West Virginia State Board of Education v. Barnette*, 319 U.S. 624.

126 Maimon Schwarzschild, op. cit.

127 See https://www.law.cornell.edu/supremecourt/text/319/624

128 Maimon Schwarzschild, op. cit.

129 Ibid.

130 See https://california.public.law/codes/ca educ_code_section_51500

131 Orange County Department of Education, "Special Community Forums on 'California's Ethnic Study Model Curriculum,'" January 5, 2022, available at https://ocbe.us/Documents/Board%20Updates/Policy%20Paper%20on%20Ethnic%20Studies%20and%20Critical%20Race%20Theory%20in%20California.pdf

132 Kimberly Sellery, "Orange County Board of Education Denounces Critical Race Theory, Discusses Ethnic Studies," August 6, 2021, available at http://blog.csba.org/oc-board-forum-crt/

133 California School Board Association, op. cit.

134 Ibid.

135 Ibid.

136 Andrew Atterbury, "Indian River schools, NAACP clear path toward resolving 51-year-old desegregation order," *Treasure Coast Newspapers*, August 24, 2018, https://www.tcpalm.com/story/news/education/indian-river-county-schools/2018/08/24/indian-river-county-schools-announce-major-desegregation-order-move/1074523002/.

137 Hannah Grossman, "California school official denounces 'mixed-race' dad as a 'White male' for probing equity course: complaint," *Fox News*, June 21, 2022, https://www.foxnews.com/media/california-school-official-mixed-race-dad-white-male-probing-radical-equity-course-complaint.

138 "Governor Ron DeSantis Signs Historic Bill to Protect Parental Rights in Education," March 28, 2022, https://flgov.com/2022/03/28/governor-ron-desantis-signs-historic-bill-to-protect-parental-rights-in-education/.

139 Corinne Murdock, "Moms for Liberty Williamson County Lays Bare Evidence of Critical Race Theory, Suicide Ideation, Violence, and More in Curriculum Across 33 Counties," The Tennessee Star, June 16, 2021, https://tennesseestar.com/2021/06/16/moms-for-liberty-williamson-county-lays-bare-evidence-of-critical-race-theory-suicide-ideation-violence-and-more-in-curriculum-across-33-counties/.

140 Evan McMorris-Santoro and Meridith Edwards, "Tennessee parents say some books make students 'feel discomfort' because they're White. They say a new law backs them up," CNN, September 29, 2021. https://www.cnn.com/2021/09/29/us/tennessee-law-hb-580-book-debate/index.html.

141 "Promoting Patriotism and Pride in American History," 1776 Project Pac, https://1776projectpac.com/, accessed October 27, 2022.

142 "Who Votes for Mayor?" http://whovotesformayor.org/about.

143 Jinghong Cai, "The Public's Voice," *The National School Boards Association*, April 1, 2020, https://www.nsba.org/ASBJ/2020/April/the-publics-voice.

144 "County of San Diego: San Dieguito Union HS Special Vacancy Election, November 2, 2021," https://www.sdvote.com/content/dam/rov/en/pdf/special-elections-2021/4228bulletin1.pdf.

145 Ballotpedia, "School board elections, 2021," https://ballotpedia.org/School_board_elections,_2021#California.

146 Emily Crane, "'Woke' warriors on San Fran school board deny gay white dad with bi-racial daughter place on volunteer parent committee because he's not diverse ENOUGH," *Daily Mail*, February 11, 2021, https://www.dailymail.co.uk/news/article-9249807/Gay-white-dad-denied-spot-San-Francisco-school-boards-parent-council.html.

147 Katy Grimes, "SF School Board's Fast-Track Resolution to Eliminate Merit-Based Admission to Lowell High School," February 10, 2021, *California Globe*, https://californiaglobe.com/articles/sf-school-boards-fast-track-resolution-to-eliminate-merit-based-admission-to-lowell-high-school/.

148 Joanne Jacobs, "School Board Shakeup in San Francisco," *Education Next*, May 24, 2022, https://www.educationnext.org/school-board-shakeup-san-francisco-arrogance-incompetence-woke-rhetoric-trigger-successful-recall-effort/.

149 Jill Tucker, "These are the 44 schools S.F. is renaming. Which would you have changed?" *San Francisco Chronicle*, https://www.sfchronicle.com/projects/2021/school-name-poll/.

150 Vanessa Romo, "San Francisco School Board Rescinds Controversial School Renaming Plan," *NPR*, April 7, 2021, https://www.npr.org/2021/04/07/984919925/san-francisco-school-board-rescinds-controversial-school-renaming-plan.

151 Wenyuan Wu, "Can We 'Long March' Back through the Institutions?" *Minding the Campus*, May 9, 2022, https://www.mindingthecampus.org/2022/05/09/can-we-long-march-back-through-the-institutions/.

152 Ryan Girdusky, "How I'm fighting for school boards," *The Washington Examiner*, June 9, 2021, https://www.washingtonexaminer.com/opinion/how-im-fighting-for-school-boards.

153 Kelly Weill, "Far-Right Snitch Network Targets Schools That Talk Race," *The Daily Beast*, June 11, 2021, https://www.thedailybeast.com/critical-race-theory-panic-sees-far-right-snitch-network-target-schools-that-talk-race.

154 Tommy Keeler Jr. "Barlow, Gutshall and Rutz win Shenandoah County School Board seats," *The Northern Virginia Daily*, November 3, 2021, https://www.nvdaily.com/nvdaily/barlow-gutshall-and-rutz-win-shenandoah-county-school-board-seats/article_bf5a04d0-d87d-50ea-a9ac-2e967ec53126.html.

155 Tim Carpenter, "Seven of 10 Kansas school board candidates backed by 1776 PAC win," *Kansas Reflector*, November 3, 2021, https://kansasreflector.com/briefs/eight-of-10-kansas-school-board-candidates-backed-by-1776-project-pac-win/.

156 Timothy Bella, "Conservative-led school board fires superintendent after allegations of private ultimatum, teacher protest,"
The Washington Post, February 5, 2022, https://www.wash-
ingtonpost.com/education/2022/02/05/colorado-conserva-
tive-school-board-fires-superintendent/.

157 https://www.christianpost.com/news/anti-crt-candi-
dates-flip-school-board-majorities-across-florida.html

158 Stephane Courtois, et al, *The Black Book of Communism* (Cam-
bridge, MA: Harvard Press), p. 517.

ACKNOWLEDGMENTS

Many people assisted in the preparation of this book. The authors would especially like to thank Frank Xu and Ted Richards.

The authors would also like to thank Pacific Research Institute president and CEO Sally Pipes. In addition, they thank PRI senior vice president Rowena Itchon, and PRI communications director Tim Anaya for editing this book (any remaining errors and omissions are the sole responsibilities of the authors). Thanks also go to graphic designer Dana Beigel, PRI vice president of development Ben Smithwick, and the other dedicated staff who made this book possible.

The authors of this book worked independently. Their views and conclusions do not necessarily represent those of the board, supporters, and staff of PRI.

ABOUT THE **Authors**

Lance Izumi is Senior Director of the Center for Education at the Pacific Research Institute. He has written and produced numerous books, studies, and films on a wide variety of education topics. His articles have appeared in a wide variety of national, international, and academic publications.

Most recently, he is the author of the 2021 PRI book *The Homeschool Boom: Pandemic, Policies, and Possibilities* and the 2019 PRI book *Choosing Diversity: How Charter Schools Promote Diverse Learning Models and Meet the Diverse Needs of Parents and Children.*

He is a former two-term president of the Board of Governors of the California Community Colleges, the largest system of higher education in the nation, and served as a member of the Board from 2004 to 2015.

He served as a commissioner on the California Postsecondary Education Commission and as a member of the United States Civil Rights Commission's California Advisory Committee.

Lance received his Juris Doctorate from the University of Southern California School of Law, his Master of Arts in political science from the University of California at Davis, and his Bachelor of Arts in economics and history from the University of California at Los Angeles.

Wenyuan Wu holds a Ph.D. in International Studies from the University of Miami and is the Executive Director of Californians for Equal Rights Foundation. She previously served in the same capacity for the historic No on 16 Campaign. Dr. Wu has been interviewed by the *Wall Street Journal*, Fox News,

National Review, NBC News, ABC News, NPR, Quartz, *Ed Source*, College Fix and others. She writes for Minding the Campus of the National Association of Scholars, the *Epoch Times* and other premium outlets. She also sits on the board of Parents Defending Education Action and advises Color Us United as well as Parents Defending Education.

Since late 2020, she has focused her advocacy and research work on combatting the intrusion of critical race theory (CRT) in American public life. In addition to participating in high-profile public speaking engagements on the topic and giving expert testimony in various state legislature hearings, she and her team launched a website (www.rejectcrt.org) to provide practical resources for everyday Americans facing CRT. She also authored a booklet on CRT in spring 2021 and organized a bipartisan and multi-racial coalition against CRT.

McKenzie Richards is a Policy Associate at Pacific Research Institute where she researches and writes on issues pertaining to education reform and health care policy.

Additionally, Richards is a 2021-2022 Stand Together Fellow in Health Care Policy and an Intercollegiate Studies Institute Honors Scholar. She is a recipient of the Richard and Helen DeVos Leadership Award for her work in education.

She holds a Bachelor of Arts in Political Science from Brigham Young University. She is pursuing a master's degree at the School of Public Policy at Pepperdine University.

Pacific Research Institute

The Pacific Research Institute (PRI) champions freedom, opportunity, and personal responsibility by advancing free-market policy solutions. It provides practical solutions for the policy issues that impact the daily lives of all Americans, and demonstrates why the free market is more effective than the government at providing the important results we all seek: good schools, quality health care, a clean environment, and a robust economy.

Founded in 1979 and based in San Francisco, PRI is a non-profit, non-partisan organization supported by private contributions. Its activities include publications, public events, media commentary, community leadership, legislative testimony, and academic outreach.

Center for Business and Economics

PRI shows how the entrepreneurial spirit—the engine of economic growth and opportunity—is stifled by onerous taxes, regulations, and lawsuits. It advances policy reforms that promote a robust economy, consumer choice, and innovation.

Center for Education

PRI works to restore to all parents the basic right to choose the best educational opportunities for their children. Through research and grassroots outreach, PRI promotes parental choice in education, high academic standards, teacher quality, charter schools, and school-finance reform.

Center for the Environment

PRI reveals the dramatic and long-term trend toward a cleaner, healthier environment. It also examines and promotes the essential ingredients for abundant resources and environmental quality: property rights, markets, local action, and private initiative.

Center for Health Care

PRI demonstrates why a single-payer Canadian model would be detrimental to the health care of all Americans. It proposes market-based reforms that would improve affordability, access, quality, and consumer choice.

Center for California Reform

The Center for California Reform seeks to reinvigorate California's entrepreneurial self-reliant traditions. It champions solutions in education, business, and the environment that work to advance prosperity and opportunity for all the state's residents.

Center for Medical Economics and Innovation

The Center for Medical Economics and Innovation aims to educate policymakers, regulators, health care professionals, the media, and the public on the critical role that new technologies play in improving health and accelerating economic growth.

Free Cities Center

The Free Cities Center cultivates innovative ideas to improve our cities and urban life based around freedom and property rights – not government.